BOUND

BOUND

Over 20 Artful Handmade Books

ERICA EKREM

LARK

DEDICATION

This book is for my grandmother, who instilled in me her love of books,
and for my children, Eden and Natteo, the greatest pair of storytellers I'll ever know.

An Imprint of Sterling Publishing
387 Park Avenue South
New York, NY 10016

Text © 2015 by Erica Ekrem
Illustrations by Sue Havens
Photography by Satya Curcio Photography

ISBN 978-1-4547-0867-4

Library of Congress Cataloging-in-Publication Data

Ekrem, Erica.
  Bound : over 20 artful handmade books / Erica Ekrem.
    pages cm
  ISBN 978-1-4547-0867-4 (paperback)
  1. Bookbinding--Handbooks, manuals, etc. 2. Book design--Handbooks, manuals, etc. I. Title.
  Z271.E38 2014
  686.3--dc23
                            2013049059

Distributed in Canada by Sterling Publishing
c/o Canadian Manda Group, 165 Dufferin Street
Toronto, Ontario, Canada M6K 3H6
Distributed in the United Kingdom by GMC Distribution Services
Castle Place, 166 High Street, Lewes, East Sussex, England BN7 1XU
Distributed in Australia by Capricorn Link (Australia) Pty. Ltd.
P.O. Box 704, Windsor, NSW 2756, Australia

For information about custom editions, special sales, and premium and corporate purchases,
please contact Sterling Special Sales at 800-805-5489 or specialsales@sterlingpublishing.com.

Manufactured in China

4 6 8 10 9 7 5 3

larkcrafts.com

CONTENTS

INTRODUCTION

I have always felt deeply connected to books. There exists a photo of me barely clothed, maybe five years old, sitting beneath the summer sun inside a storybook large enough to swallow me whole. In fact, I rarely remember a time in my life when I wasn't fascinated by an exotic world painted by the well-crafted words of a new author I had discovered.

My early childhood was painted in the magic of fairy tales with glimmering watercolors of 1940s storybook illustrations from previous generations. A few years later, when I began to decode written language, the first words I read were in a musty set of Dick and Jane books my grandmother had collected. As a tween, I devoted myself religiously to a diary, creating a memoir of my likes and dislikes, filing away my first kisses and heartaches. As I grew older, my storyline began to take the form of prose, poetry, and stream-of-consciousness writing influenced by voices like Anaïs Nin, Jim Morrison, and Ken Kesey.

It wasn't long before I left my hometown, enrolled in university courses, and began exploring philosophy and spiritual texts. Wherever I found myself, undoubtedly there were books at hand. Finally, after a few years (and universities), I stumbled upon a prerequisite course that altered my path, and curiously enough, melded my studies together—it was a class that taught me how to design and build books.

In 2004, after I completed my studies and lovingly repeated the bookbinding course as many times as I could, I wished for two things in my life: to live in a forest and to bind books. I serendipitously found a cabin in the woods, as well as Bison Bookbinding and Letterpress in the nearby town of Bellingham, which graciously hired me.

By that time I had been experimenting with my own materials and bookbinding techniques. I gathered secondhand materials from thrift stores and salvage boxes. Soon after, I was asked to sell the journals in a local shop, and then finally I embarked on selling on Etsy. That's when I realized it was possible to make a living doing what I loved to do. From then on, I continued to explore the structure of the bound book, searching for the creative edge where beauty meets utility.

And now, thirty some years after that sunlit photo of me inside my colossal book, I find myself immersed in my biggest project yet: this book. In some ways it *has* swallowed me, by captivating my attention the way only a good storybook can.

I invite you to think of this book as a bookbinding course. I want to offer a resource, to give you a good foundation, inspire you, fuel your creativity, and spark your ideas. I often ask: How beautiful and functional can a book be? This is the question that moved me to write this book and one that I hope will be meaningful to you.

In this book, I've provided simple modifications on basic stitches and new stitching techniques that I've developed to aid you in integrating up-cycled and found cover materials. For those of you new to bookbinding, if at first the projects seem challenging, I urge you to keep practicing. The more you handle the materials and intuit the way they want to be handled, the easier it will become. You might begin with the simple bindings such as the pamphlet stitch and work your way up to a more complex combination of stitches.

For those of you who are more experienced, I challenge you to approach these projects with a beginner's mind. You never know what new pathway you may discover! And for those of you who like to cross-pollinate your skillset, I've incorporated traditional sewing techniques such as embroidery and machine sewing, as well as integrating wood-burning, beachcombing, and botanical pressing.

My love and deep appreciation for the earth cannot go unspoken here. I owe much, if not all, of my success in bookbinding to the creative impulses and visions I've received by connecting with the natural world. In return, it is my hope to give back to nature by taking the time to seek tools and materials that are sustainable and durable enough to last a lifetime, or in the least, ones that will leave a light environmental footprint. In this way, the hand-stitched books I make become a silent ode of thanks and appreciation for the natural abundance in my life.

I urge you to spend time in your part of the world, wherever you are—be it city, rural countryside, forest, urban park, or beach—and let nature speak to you. Take my techniques that I have developed over many years and use them to inform your one-of-a-kind pieces. I ask that if you use any of my techniques in a commercial way, that it be in the context of your very own unique art. Express your love of books as I have done. And never be afraid to be swallowed, however momentarily, by the beauty you create.

—Erica Ekrem

THE BASICS: MATERIALS, TOOLS, AND TECHNIQUES

INTRODUCTION

In the following pages, I bring you 21 book structures made with materials sourced from places as local as your backyard to more global offerings via the online marketplace. As you explore this book, let the use of materials spark your imagination and allow the magic of the old world guide you to a slower pace of being. If you aren't already, I hope you will begin to explore the materials found in your own unique and precious natural environment and enable Nature to guide you in your creative process. Most of all, have fun and be curious! This is how I discovered the projects within.

SOURCES

You can get your bookbinding supplies from various places, depending upon the kind of materials you like to work with.

Stores

Many of the materials for the projects in this book can be found in your local craft or art store. Check out your local shops first. If you don't find everything you need, source your materials from a specialty bookbinding store that offers online shopping. See page 141 for a list of retailers.

Upcycling and Repurposing

If you prefer your materials to have an Old World charm and a history of their own, consider visiting a local thrift store, or peruse the out-of-circulation bins at your nearest library and bookstore. I've discovered many beautiful materials via secondhand sources, including antique book covers that were beautifully printed by artisans now long gone. Before deconstructing an antique book, make sure it is not a rare book or one of historical value. You can look online to determine a book's approximate value, but to be sure, choose volumes that are beyond repair or of low value, such as vintage textbooks. See page 19 for more on deconstructing a vintage book.

Harvesting Natural Materials

Perhaps the most pleasurable location to find natural materials is in your own backyard or the greater outdoors. I comb the nearest beaches for driftwood planks and clamshells. I am always careful not to disturb the wildlife, and I take nothing that is alive. Be sure you know the local laws, specifically whether natural materials are permitted to be harvested from the land, especially in land preserves or other protected environments.

MATERIALS

You can be innovative when it comes to materials for constructing books, but below are some materials you will most likely need.

Paper

Paper is the magic ingredient of any hand-stitched book. Since there is a huge range of papers to choose from, I've made a basic list of specific types that I use consistently in my books and a short guide to the specifications for each one.

Writing or text-weight paper is a light- to medium-weight paper that is usually between 35 and 80 lbs. It can be easily grouped into four to eight sheets and folded into signatures. Ideally it has a smooth and versatile surface that will allow for a variety of writing utensils, such as a ballpoint pen, pencil, or even an old-fashioned dip or fountain pen. Most importantly, it needs to be strong enough to be punched with an awl and hold thread without easily tearing.

Decorative paper lends character to your book. It is most often used in the front and back of the book to line the covers and for end sheets. There is a wide range of decorative papers to choose from, including reproductions of vintage prints, upcycled maps, marbled paper, and machine-made velvet paper. The thickness of the paper ranges from light to heavy weight. The most important factor is that it is pliable enough to handle a crisp fold yet thick enough to hold a thin coat of adhesive.

Handmade paper is usually created from natural fibers and can give your book a warm, rustic, and tactile quality. Often the edges of the paper are deckled, meaning they have an organic raw edge as opposed to a straight, trimmed edge. When using marbled paper, I like to feature the deckled edge whenever possible. For usage, handmade paper is wonderful for pages in the text block if the surface is smooth enough for writing; otherwise it can be a decorative element like an end sheet.

Handmade papers from all over the world are available for purchase at your local art store and online. Lokta paper, made from the daphne bushes in Nepal, is one of the most versatile papers to work with and a great choice if you are new to bookbinding. It comes in a variety of colors, sheet sizes, and weights. Additionally, consider seeking out and supporting a papermaker in your area. They may be using fibers that are native to your environment and may offer a paper that will contribute a unique, local nuance to your bound book.

Mixed media paper can be anything from newspaper clippings to pages torn from a discarded vintage book. Consider reusing and upcycling old wallpaper, photographs,

From top to bottom: Heavyweight lokta paper, recycled writing paper, cardstock, binder's board, wood board, cardboard, light-weight lokta paper, decorative paper, decorative paper, handmade Comfrey paper, Otomi bark paper, handmade paper.

materials that are designated as "lignin-free," "acid-free," or "pH neutral."

Leather

A leather-bound journal speaks of Old World beauty and utility. Leather as a cover material has stood the test of time and makes a journal travel-worthy by protecting the text block from the elements and general wear and tear. When sourcing leather for wraparound covers, I recommend using cowhide leather that is 3 to 5 ounces so the leather will hold its shape and provide structure to protect the text block. (Leather thickness is usually measured in ounces.)

Many of the projects in this book feature stoned oil cowhide, which has a rich, aged look to it, but you should choose the type of finish that you like best. Feel free to experiment with the raw leather edges by positioning the *live edge* at the end of the wraparound cover for a more rustic look. (*Live edge* is a term for the raw edge of a piece of leather or wood that is left as-is, or unrefined.)

If you will be adhering the leather to a cover board, I recommend choosing a lightweight leather or suede that is in the 1- to 2-ounce range. It will be easier to apply the thin leather to a board and create a smoother wraparound edge on the back of the boards. After your leather book begins to show wear, you may wish to recondition the leather with a natural leather salve or balm. A wide range of leather and leather products can be sourced in regional specialty stores and online (see Resources on page 141).

Keep in mind that even though leather is a material with many benefits, its production (which involves a chemical process) can strongly impact the environment and natural water sources. I'd recommend seeking out local artisan tanners who use natural tanning methods (vegetable tanned and brain tanned to name a couple), and upcycling leather whenever possible.

playing cards, and postcards. These papers are most often used for decorative purposes, such as end sheets and decorative spine tabs, and can even be adhered to board for making covers.

Cardstock is a thick paper primarily used for single pages in a scrapbook or photo album. It is usually has a weight of 80 lb. or more and can be folded one sheet at a time. Many of the projects in the book use cardstock to make templates and punching guides.

Archival-quality paper is acid-free or pH neutral and used by historians and artists because of its long life and ability to preserve color and ink well. You may choose to use archival materials (paper, board, and glue) if you wish your book and contents to last for generations. Look for

Board

Board is essential to making a classic hardcover book. Below are a few types of board and their uses.

Binder's board is a commonly used by bookbinders. It is acid-free and comes in a range of thicknesses. I choose a thin $\frac{1}{16}$-inch (1.6 mm) board for most of my small- to medium-sized books because it is easy to cut by hand or with a small guillotine paper cutter. Another traditional board I use is black, acid-free **museum board**. Often I cover the front and back of the boards with decorative paper and leave the edges raw so the black color is exposed. It ranges from $\frac{1}{32}$- to $\frac{1}{16}$-inch (0.8 to 1.6 mm) thick and is easy to cut by hand. Both of these boards can be found in an art or specialty bookbinding store.

Used books can be an abundant, inexpensive source of book board. You'll find that several of the projects call for a used book cover. I'll show you how to deconstruct an old book (see page 19) and reuse the board as well as the book's original cloth covering. Intercepting discarded books on the way to the dump is a great way to keep materials from going to waste. Ask your librarian or bookstore owner if they have a discard box that you can salvage your materials from. Thrift stores, yard sales, and estate sales are sources worth checking out as well.

The most protective and strong board used for bookbinding is solid **wood board**. Often, the board is not covered, so the beauty of the wood grain can be appreciated. You can find board available in sheets at your local hardware store. I prefer a solid wood board that is about $\frac{3}{16}$-inch (5 mm) thick with a raw or unfinished surface. Be sure the wood you choose is a hardwood that has been dried so that it will not curl or warp after you have bound it. Always position the grain of the wood horizontally on your cover to decrease the chance of it cracking along the grain.

To cut your board to size, you will need a simple handsaw; a wood drill is used to make the holes for attaching the boards to the text block. An alternative source for wood is a local beach, if you live near one. I'm always surprised at the amount of used milled boards I've found along the shoreline. I especially like to pick up boards that have paint or nails on them as both are ways to recycle and clean the beach. Again, always be sure to check the local laws on beachcombing and make sure you can legally remove material from the beach.

Closures

There are more than a couple ways to ensure your book stays closed. Here are a few of my favorites.

Heavy-duty metal snaps are a secure method of protecting the contents of your book. They come in a range of sizes and metal types and can be purchased online or at most leather shops. Most often, I use *line 24* in an antique brass color. (*Line 24* refers to the size of the snap.) If this is your first time using snaps, you will need a manual snap setter and a leather hole punch. Also have a hammer and wooden scrap board available for setting the snap. There are a few different methods for setting a snap, so ask the clerk at the store for a snap-setting kit and how-to instructions. Be ready to practice on a leather scrap until you can set the snap correctly before attaching it to your finished book.

Buttons are a simple, easy method of securing your book closed. You may wish to purchase a new button or upcycle a used one. I find the best type of button has two to four holes and a flat back. Use strong button or binder's thread to secure the button to the cover. If you are not experienced with attaching buttons, there are plenty of online instructionals to learn from! Also, consider making your own button from clay, wood, or stone using a drill and drill bit that is appropriate to the material to make the holes.

Leather ties are a classic way to close a leather-bound book. You can find thin leather latigo (straps) at leather specialty shops and online. You can also make your own leather tie by cutting a long $\frac{3}{8}$-inch-wide (9.5 mm) strip of matching leather and sewing it to the cover. Wrap the strip around the outside of the journal once or twice and tuck it securely beneath the wrapped strip to secure.

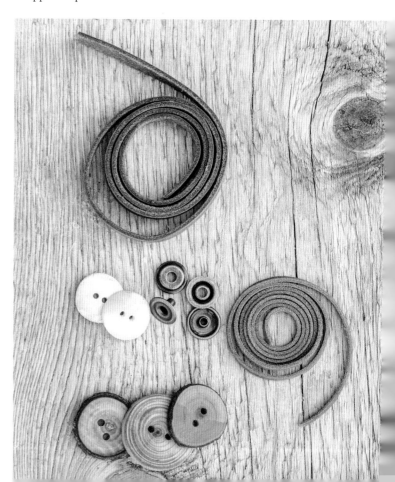

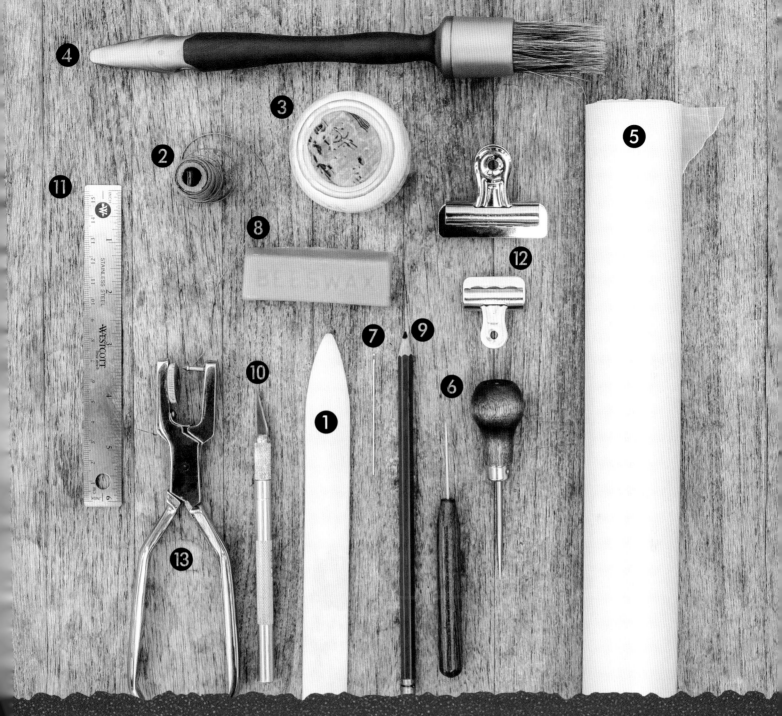

Basic Toolkit

You will see that each project calls for the "Basic Bookmaking Toolkit." This refers to the following essentials:

1. Bone folder

2. Binder's thread

3. Glue

4. Glue brush

5. Wax paper

6. Awls

7. Needle

8. Beeswax

9. Pencil

10. Craft knife

11. Metal ruler

12. Rubber bands and binder clamps

13. Hole punch

Not pictured: scissors, paper cutter, cutting mat, phonebook

TOOLS

Below you will find a list of very basic tools you'll almost always need, along with a short list of optional tools.

Bone Folder

A bookbinding essential that is traditionally made of polished bone. It is pressed along a fold line to create an even, crisp fold. They are available in many sizes and shapes.

Binder's Thread

Binder's thread holds it all together. High-quality, archival bookbinding thread is made from linen, an extremely strong, durable fiber derived from the flax plant. It is available in a variety of thickness, or plies: 18/3 or 12/3 ply is adequate for general bookbinding and all the projects featured here. (These are relatively thick plies.) Linen thread is available waxed or unwaxed. Often, the prewaxed thread is thicker than I prefer and coated with petroleum-based wax, so I purchase unwaxed thread and coat it myself by running it over a block of natural beeswax (page 18). You may also consider other non-elastic threads such as buttonhole thread, hemp thread, and upholstery thread. For more delicate bindings, experiment with metallic thread, embroidery floss, or even a natural fiber yarn.

Glue

Polyvinyl acetate glue (PVA) is a common paper glue that dries quickly and clear. It is water-based so it will easily clean up with warm, soapy water. Another traditional binding glue is all-natural wheat paste. Both are available from most art stores and specialty bookbinding shops.

Glue Brush

To spread glue onto the materials, use a small, round-tipped glue brush, or you can also get by with an inexpensive flat-head brush. Immediately after use, be sure to rinse it with warm, soapy water and then dry the bristles with a cotton cloth or hang it, brush side down, to air-dry.

Wax Paper

This is useful while applying glue to your paper materials. It protects your work surface from becoming sticky and allows for a quick and easy cleanup during and after applying glue. It is available by the roll and is commonly found in grocery stores.

Awls

Awls are used for punching holes in paper as well as in cover boards. Traditionally, an awl is made from a thin, tapered metal shaft with a wooden handle. You may also use a large safety pin, upholstery needle, T-pin, or a thin, sharp nail.

Needles

Use a small-eyed, blunt bookbinding needle to sew your punched signatures. The points are blunt so they won't inadvertently pierce or scratch the paper—or you. Thin, strong needles are ideal for fitting through small holes in the signatures and often can be found at a specialty binding shop.

Beeswax

Beeswax is used to coat raw binder's thread. It protects thread from friction, allows it to glide more freely through the holes, and creates knots that are less likely to slip. (See page 18 for more.)

Pencil

A simple number 2 pencil is used for making marks. Be sure to have a sharpener on hand.

Craft Knife

A craft knife can be used for cutting lightweight material such as book board. It is made of a metal handle with a replaceable sharp triangular blade.

Metal Ruler

Rulers are extremely useful for measuring, and they are also used to draw straight lines. A large 18-inch (45.7 cm) metal-edge ruler with a no-slip cork backing is most effective. For smaller projects, consider a shorter 6-inch (15.2 cm) metal ruler.

Scissors

A sharp pair of scissors is indispensable. A small pair is best for trimming the threads in hard-to-reach places, while a large pair is effective for general use and for cutting paper.

Paper Cutter

A couple of options are available: a guillotine (swinging-arm cutter) has a gridded baseboard with a bladed arm that swings down to chop the paper. The other variant is a rotary cutter, which has a sliding shuttle with a rotating circular blade that slices the paper.

Hole Punch

Hole punches are used for punching neat, clean holes through thicker materials such as leather and binder's board. They come in a variety of styles such as rotary, hollow punch, or screw punch and offer a wide range of hole sizes. Most often, I reach for my hand-held rotary punch as it is the most versatile and the hole size adjusts with a simple rotation of the wheel.

Rubber Bands and Binder Clamps

These are used for holding sheets or stacks of paper together and keeping the signatures in order. A variety of sizes will be needed to accommodate the variable thickness of stacks.

Cutting Mat

A self-healing cutting mat protects your work surface and provides a surface for cutting with a craft or utility knife. Eco-friendly alternatives include a sheet of cardboard or an old wooden tabletop that can handle wear and tear.

Phonebook or Punching Cradle

A phonebook or punching cradle is handy to have for punching holes in signatures. It nests the fold of the signature's spine to keep the sheets of paper neatly together, and it provides protection so you're not damaging your work surface—or your hands!—each time you punch your awl through. (See page 17 for more on punching holes in signatures.)

Corner Rounder

This handy tool is used to punch the corners of paper to create a rounded edge. It is entirely optional, but it adds a nice touch to a handmade book. Handheld rounders are available, but if you intend to cut more than a couple of sheets at a time, consider investing in a heavy-duty tabletop rounder. Though more expensive, their performance is worth every penny.

Additional Tools Needed

Electric drill with wood and diamond bits
Leather hole punch
Paintbrush
Drafting compass
Dust mask
Safety glasses
Handsaw
Pressing iron
Books, weights, or a book press
Small water tub
Sewing machine
Sandpaper
Embroidery and Button Needles

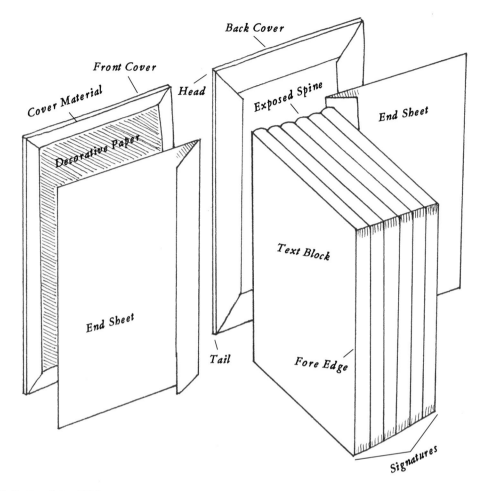

Back Cover

Front Cover

Cover Material

Head

Exposed Spine

End Sheet

Decorative Paper

End Sheet

Text Block

Tail

Fore Edge

Signatures

BASIC TECHNIQUES

Throughout the book, I will refer back to techniques instructed and illustrated in this section.

Making a Text Block

The text block is the foundation of the book, and how you intend to use the book will determine how you make it. For example, you might want to fill your book with scrapbook or photo album pages; or if you want to use it as a journal, you'll need to be sure and use paper you can easily write on. Each signature may have wraparound sheets made of decorative paper or fabric, and maybe only the first and last signatures have end sheets. There is plenty of room for creativity.

Folding Signatures

The first thing you must do is decide whether to fold with the grain or against the grain. In traditional book arts, binders are taught to fold *with* the grain of the paper—that is, with the grain running parallel to the spine. This has several benefits: easier folding, pages that turn more readily, and less likelihood

of the text block warping and compromising the strength of the binding. By all means, if you wish to go with the grain, be assured it is a time-proven method with obvious benefits.

On the contrary, I offer this perspective: In our time of diminishing natural resources (i.e., forests and clean water), I believe it vitally important to upcycle and reuse as often as possible, especially in the realm of paper products. When I was sourcing paper for the projects in this book, I sought out upcycled paper. It was abundant, but not usually in adequate quantity or sizes to allow for folding with the grain. So I choose to be eco-conscientious, and I often folded against the grain and used less paper than I might have if I had folded with the grain. However you choose to fold, do keep it consistent: If you fold against the grain for one signature, be sure to do it for all of the signatures in the book.

1. To fold your paper into signatures, gather four or five sheets of paper that have been cut to size.

2. Align the stack by gently tapping (or jogging) the bottom and one side edge on the work surface to align the sheets.

3. Set the stack on the table and firmly press the one side of the paper to the table while you fold the other over to align with the pressed edge (A).

4. Secure both edges of the paper with one hand. With the bone folder in your other hand, gently crease the fold, beginning in the center and sliding to one end and then the other. To finish, place the bone folder in the center of the fold and complete the fold in the other direction (B).

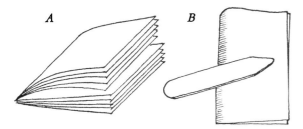

Making a Template

Many of the projects require you to make a template for punching the sewing stations (also called stations) or making a part of the book. In some cases, I've included a template that you can simply copy onto cardstock. Some templates will need to be enlarged to reach 100 percent with a photocopier or scanner (there is a label on these templates that indicates the percentage to enlarge). In cases where the measurements of the book are unknown, such as when the materials are upcycled from an old book, a template wouldn't work, so I provide measurements instead. There are a couple of ways of making templates, and the best choice depends on your available resources.

Method 1. Use your home computer and scanner or visit your local copy shop and use a photocopier. Place the page with the template face down on the scanner flatbed. Enlarge the image (if necessary) and then scan in grayscale. Print the template file onto a sheet of white cardstock. Cut the template from the cardstock.

Method 2. Use tracing paper and carbon paper. Enlarge the image (if necessary) from Method 1 above and make a template. Place a sheet of translucent tracing paper over the template and trace it with a pencil. Layer the tracing paper over a sheet of carbon paper and place both on top of the cardstock. Use a pencil to retrace the template onto the carbon paper. The carbon paper will reproduce the lines onto the cardstock. Use care to hold all papers in place so the

copy of the template remains true to size. Set the tracing and carbon paper aside. Cut the template from the cardstock.

Punching the Holes

The next step in making a text block is punching the signatures with holes, or sewing stations. Many of the projects provide detailed punching templates that will guide you in the proper placement of each sewing station. Templates are integral in creating accurately punched signatures in a time-efficient manner.

1. Make a template by cutting a piece of cardstock 3 inches (7.6 cm) wide and the exact height of the signatures. Fold it in half vertically and then measure and punch the holes in the folded edge. You may need to number the holes and label the orientation (top/bottom) of the template with an arrow if the binding is more complex. (Note that some of the more complex spine templates are already numbered for you, to help keep track of sewing stations.)

2. Open the first signature of the text block and place it in the fold of an open phonebook. Nest the open template inside the signature (in the matching top/bottom orientation) and gently punch the sewing station with an awl (A).

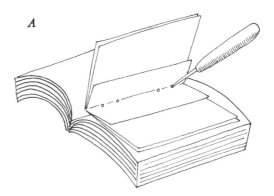

TIP: *Make the holes as small and neat as possible by using a thin awl. This is especially important in exposed spine bindings where the holes will remain visible.*

3. Continue to punch the signatures according to the project instructions. After punching the holes, be sure to stack the signatures in their proper order. You may also temporarily bind the signatures with a clip or rubber band to keep them in place until you are ready to sew.

Preparing the Cover

Cover preparation varies according to the material used. Each project will provide instructions or a template for drilling or punching the cover holes. In general, the holes for attaching the cover to the text block will be marked with a pencil according to the template and punched with the awl. However, some materials (such as wood, slate, or shell) may require a drill and bit. In either case, be sure to punch or drill the hole by starting on the outer side of the cover. This will ensure that the rough side of the puncture will be hidden on the inside of the cover.

Preparing the Binder's Thread

As I mentioned earlier, linen thread is available waxed or unwaxed. Since the prewaxed thread is thicker than I prefer and often coated with petroleum-based wax, I purchase unwaxed thread and coat it myself using natural beeswax. This protects it from fraying, keeps it from sliding out of the needle, locks the stitches, and allows it to slide more readily through the sewing stations. Beeswax also leaves behind a pleasing, delicate honey aroma.

1. To wax the thread, run it from end to end two or three times over a block of solid (room temperature) beeswax (A).

A

2. To thread the needle, run the end of the waxed thread through the eye. Do not fasten the thread by tying a knot; leave a loose tail 2 to 3 inches (5.1 to 7.6 cm) long instead.

All but one project in this book are bound with a single-threaded needle. "Single threaded" means that you put the end of the thread through the needle's eye, far enough to keep it from slipping out—perhaps a few inches (A). The stitches will be made with just one thread this way. A double-threaded needle, on the other hand, has thread passing through its eye and then doubling back on itself, the ends evened out, the same way you might do to sew a button or a hem (B). This way, each stitch is made of two threads. Little Traveler is one project in which you'll use the latter method.

A   *B*

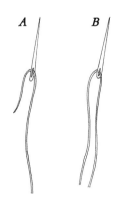

Stitching

The general stitching pattern for books with multiple signatures begins with a similar series of knots to link the heads and tails of the signature together.

1. To begin, guide the needle and thread into the first sewing station on the right. Leave a tail of thread of the recommended length on the outside of the first station. Continue sewing along the spine as directed for the particular project.

2. Once the needle has exited the last station, place the next signature beside the first and make a direct link (page 140) into the nearest sewing station. Continue sewing down the spine of the second signature as directed.

3. Once the needle has exited out the last station, you will need to link to the tail thread of the first signature with a square knot (page 28). Allow the tail thread to hang in the opposite direction away from the recently added signature.

4. Place the third signature beside the second and draw the needle and thread directly into the nearest station (A). Continue sewing down the spine of the third signature.

A

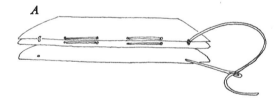

5. Once the needle has exited out the last station, link to the previous signature with a true kettle stitch (B).

B

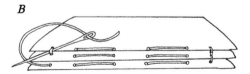

6. From here on out, use a true kettle stitch to link at both ends of each signature.

7. Finish the binding by linking to the previous signature with a true kettle stitch.

8. Leave a loose tail of thread at the end. This will be used later to attach the covers.

DECONSTRUCTING A VINTAGE HARDCOVER

A few of the projects will ask you to remove the hard cover from a used or vintage book. Again, I always check online to make sure the book is not a special edition or a high-value book before I deconstruct it. I also recommend wearing a dust mask to protect your lungs from the fine paper dust or possibly mold spores that may become airborne during disassembly. Additionally, It is a good idea to work in a ventilated area.

1. To begin, lay the book on your work surface. Open the front cover to expose the seam or hinge between the right edge of the front cover board and the first page.

2. Place a metal straightedge ruler along the left edge of the seam. Gently run a craft knife along the edge of the ruler (over the seam) from top to bottom. It may take a couple of passes to slice through the multiple layers of paper and binding material. Use care to only slice through the material on the inside of the cover; avoid slicing into the cover and spine itself. Once the front of the text block has completely separated from the front side of the cover, turn to the back of the book and expose the inside of the back cover.

3. Again, position the straightedge ruler and run the craft knife along the seam between the back cover and the spine of the text block until they separate. Once you completely slice through the layers of paper material, the text block should no longer be bound to the hard cover.

4. Remove the text block and set it aside.

5. Depending on the method used to initially bind the book, there may be a few more materials to peel away from the cover to clean it up. If you see muslin-like cloth or threads attached to the inner edges of the inside covers, carefully peel them off and discard. Also, pull away any lumpy or thick paper that was used to line the inner covers.

6. To separate the spine from the covers if that is called for, place the open cover on a cutting mat, outside facing up. Position the metal ruler on the spine panel ¼ inch (6 mm) from the front cover board. With a craft knife, cut the spine panel from the front cover by gently running the blade along the metal ruler. Reposition the ruler on the spine panel ¼ inch (6 mm) from the back cover board and repeat. (A)

Use care not to disturb the spine (it can be quite fragile). Also, do not peel away the cloth that wraps around to the edges of the cover boards. Once the cover is cleaned up, it's ready to be reincarnated into a new journal!

A

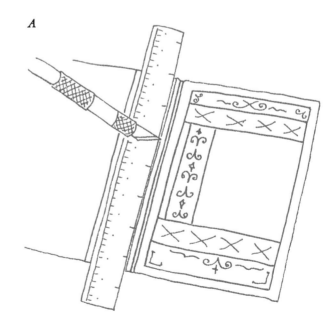

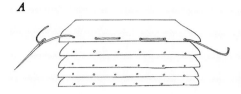

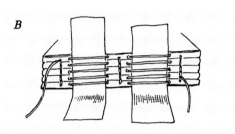

Running Stitch

This simple binding can be applied to a variety of book structures, such as an exposed spine or a book with a leather or hardcover casing. In its simplest form, it consists of a simple, straight stitch that weaves up and down the spines of the signatures (A) with true kettle stitches at the left and right stations that link the signatures.

In my projects, you'll find the running stitch is often combined with other stitches to make a strong and attractive binding. Sometimes, the stitches of multiple signatures may be gathered together (see gathering stitch, page 24) in the last signature to strengthen the binding and to add ornamentation. Tapes (rectangular tabs of paper, ribbon, or cloth) can also be sized to fit between the sewing stations on the exterior of the spine and sewn over with the running stitches (B) to further strengthen and add an ornamental quality to the binding. (See Reincarnate Journal on page 46.)

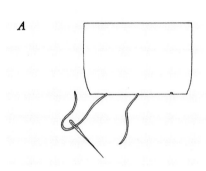

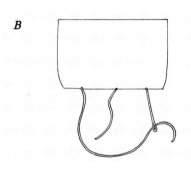

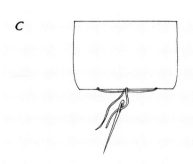

Pamphlet Stitch

This basic binding structure is a quick and simple method of binding a small book with few pages. It usually consists of one signature, but may also be applied to multiple signatures within a case to accommodate for a book with a greater thickness (see Little Traveler on page 103).

1. To make a basic pamphlet stitch, place the tip of the threaded needle in through the outside of the center sewing station and draw the thread into the center of the signature, leaving a 4- to 6-inch (10.2 to 15.2 cm) tail on the outside of the spine.

2. Guide the needle into the leftmost sewing station and pull the thread to the outside of the spine (A).

3. Draw the needle into the rightmost sewing station, skipping over the center station entirely, and pull the thread to the inside of the spine (B).

4. Complete the stitch by guiding the needle through the center station from the inside of the signature to the outside of the spine (C), or use a loop knot (page 28). Tighten all threads. Remove the needle and bind the loose ends with a square knot (page 28).

If you prefer to hide your finishing knot, the binding can also begin inside the signature, thus ending with the binding knot inside, hidden from view.

Long Stitch

This method of binding is a simple and effective way to attach the text block to a leather or cloth cover. The stitching pattern involves one long stitch that weaves in and out of the sewing stations. It is similar to the running stitch (page 20), but it does not use true kettle stitches (page 24) to link the signatures together. Rather, the long stitch links directly (page 140) from one signature to the next. Because true kettle stitches are not used, it is important that each signature is firmly attached to the cover's spine and that there is no slack in the thread. The long stitch pattern can also be modified to allow for decorative stitches such as the gathering stitch (page 24) along the outside of the spine.

Here is a general stitching pattern for long stitch (A):

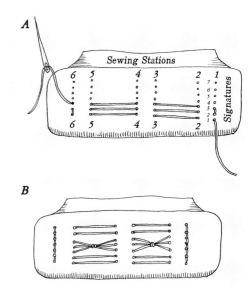

1. Signature 1: Lift the front edge of the cover and enter the threaded needle into the rightmost station (sewing station 1) of row 1 on the cover, draw it through the spine, and into the interior of the last signature of the book. Leave a 6-inch (15.2 cm) tail on the outside of the spine. Continue sewing with a continuous running stitch (page 20) through all three layers (signature, spine, and cover) until you arrive on the outside of the spine on the leftmost station (station 6, in this case). Make sure to pull the thread taut at the completion of every stitch so the binding is strong and there is no slack in the thread.

2. Signature 2: Enter into the closest hole in the next row on the outside of the cover. Pull a signature from the bottom of the stack and align it to the next row of stations within the cover. Draw the needle into the signature and pull the thread taut. Continue sewing the remaining signatures using this long stitch pattern.

3. Consider adding some gathering stitches (page 24) while sewing the fifth signature. To do this, gather the two previous signatures' threads between stations 2 and 3 and stations 4 and 5 (B).

4. Continue with the long stitch pattern to bind the remaining signatures.

5. After the last signature is attached, weave the threaded needle in and out of the top stations near the head of the spine to fill in the threadless gaps between stations. Once all gaps are filled, enter into the nearest signature and tie off (see page 27). Trim the thread ends to ¼ inch (6 mm).

6. Thread the remaining tail onto the needle and repeat step 5 at the tail of the spine.

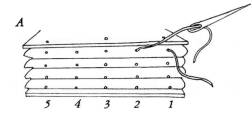

A

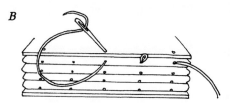

B

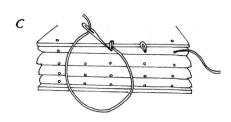

C

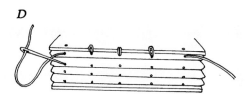

D

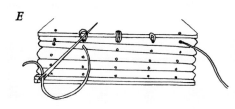

E

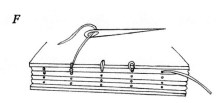

F

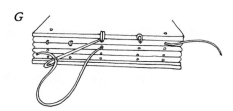

G

Coptic Stitch

This simple linking stitch creates a minimal, yet admirable, pattern on an exposed spine. A single Coptic stitch may also be called a link or chain stitch. There are several methods used to begin this stitching pattern. Since the projects in this book employing the Coptic stitch are each comprised of five or fewer stations, I've chosen a method of forming loops in the first signature that will be tightened later.

1. Begin by entering the rightmost sewing station (1) of your first signature from the outside of the spine. Draw the thread to the inside of the signature, leaving a 6- to 12-inch (15.2 to 30.5 cm) tail on the outside.

2. Draw the thread to sewing station 2 and exit (A).

3. Reenter sewing station 2 and pull the thread until a small loop forms on the outside spine of the signature. Guide the needle into the next station (3) from the inside, using care not to pull the loop out of the previous signature. Continue to the next station. (In this example, the next station is the center one, sewing station 3.) If you have a cover to fasten, pull the thread to the outside of the center station and around the outside of the center cover hole (B).

4. Loop around the cover hole twice. Tighten the threads and reenter into the center station of the signature (C).

5. Continue to the next station and make a loop on the outside of the signature like you did in step 3. At the leftmost station, direct link into the next signature and pull the thread semi-taut (D).

6. Guide the needle out of the next sewing station and through the adjacent loop of the previous signature (E).

7. Carefully pull the thread of the previous signature tight until the loop disappears. Pull the thread of the second signature taut until the linking stitch is tight (F).

8. Guide the thread back into the station it just came out of and through the center station in the second signature. Pull the needle to the outside of the book. Wrap once around the link between the first signature and the cover (G), and return the needle to the center station of the second signature (H).

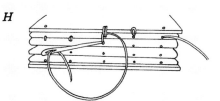

H

9. Continue to the next sewing station from inside the second signature, and link through the previous signature's loop (I).

10. Again tighten the loop by pulling the thread of the first signature toward the bottom until the loop disappears. Tighten the thread of the second signature and reenter through the hole (J).

I

11. At station 1, link to the previous signature using a square knot (page 28).

12. Continue adding signatures by linking the newest stations to the previous one with a Coptic stitch around the adjacent link at each station (J). Link the bottom and top stations of the signatures together using a true kettle stitch (page 24).

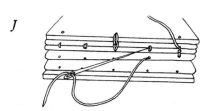

J

13. In the final signature, link the center station to the previous signature first, then guide the needle through the recently made Coptic stitch and pull the thread taut (K).

14. Place the remaining cover on the text block (L).

15. Guide the needle around the cover spine and into the center cover hole (M). Pull it through to wrap the thread around the cover spine. Loop the thread around the cover spine again (N) and pull the thread taut.

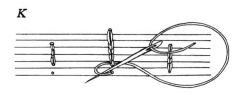

K

16. Guide the needle back into the middle station of the signature.

17. Continue the binding with a regular Coptic stitch in the next station, just like before.

Complete the binding of the text block by linking the top of the signatures with a true kettle stitch. To complete the book, see Attaching the Covers (page 25).

L

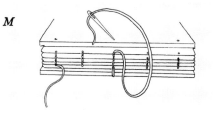

M

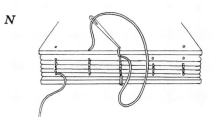

N

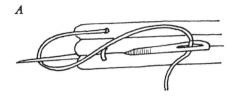

A

True Kettle Stitch

Of all the stitches, this is the one that, when performed correctly, brings the most structure to your bindings. The true kettle stitch is used to link the heads and tails of the signatures together. To do this, guide the needle under the stitch that links the previous signatures, starting from the inside of the spine and pulling the needle toward the outside left or right of the spine. Continue to pull the thread until there is a small loop remaining. Guide the needle through the loop and tighten the stitch, pulling toward the most recent signature so the needle will easily point into the next signature (A).

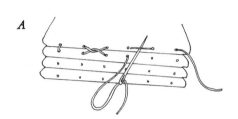

A

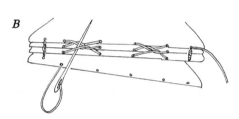

B

French Stitch

This Old World stitch is an elegant way of linking signatures along an exposed spine.

1. Begin with a running stitch (page 20) along the spine of the first signature.

2. Add the second signature and draw the needle directly into the adjacent hole in the second signature to link.

3. Continue with a running stitch that wraps once around the previous signature's long stitch (A).

4. Always tighten the thread before linking the next signature with a true kettle stitch (page 24).

5. In the following signatures, continue to wrap around the closest leg of the previous signature's thread. The French pattern will begin to emerge as you add signatures to the sewn spine (B).

A

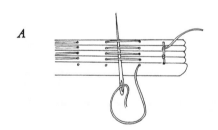

B

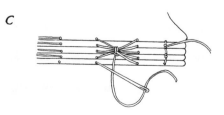

C

Gathering Stitch

A gathering stitch may be used to strengthen a long (page 21) or running (page 20) stitch binding by linking multiple signatures together. This stitch is often made while stitching the final signature of books that contain from five to nine signatures. If you are making a thicker book with more signatures, you may gather the stitches on the fifth signature and again gather the next five signatures on the tenth signature.

1. Pull the thread to the outside of the signature. Guide the needle beneath the long stitches of the previous signatures (A) and pull the thread back toward the final signature.

2. Loop beneath the thread near the current sewing station and pull the thread tight until all threads gather and a knot is formed. Be sure to center the knot between the sewing stations (B).

3. Reinforce the stitch by repeating this knot around all threads. Pull tight and enter into the next sewing station (C).

Attaching the Covers

Often, though not always, a book's covers are attached during the sewing of the text block. For exposed spine bindings, I've found it easiest to attach the head and tail of the covers after the spine is sewn. To accommodate, I always leave 10 to 12 inches (25.4 to 30.5 cm) of loose thread at the beginning and end of the binding or the length recommended in the individual projects. The method shown here will work for books with an odd number of signatures. For an even number of signatures, see the instructions on page 26.

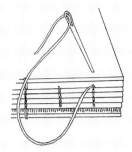

1. If the cover isn't already in place after the final signatures are linked, set it in place.

2. Thread the needle with the loose end of thread hanging from the rightmost sewing station, and then guide it around the outside of the spine and into the hole on the top of the cover (A).

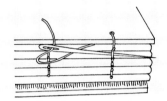

3. Draw the needle down and around the outside of the spine and pull the thread taut. Loop the needle around the linking stitch at the head of the previous signatures (B) and pull the thread taut.

4. Again, guide the thread toward the top of the cover and into the hole (C).

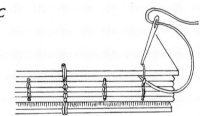

5. Draw the needle down and around the outside of the spine and pull the thread taut (D).

6. Loop the needle a second time around the linking stitch of the signatures (E) and pull the thread taut.

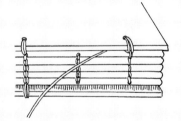

7. Continue to move the needle and thread down the linking stitches toward the back cover by using a simple technique I call hiking. Hiking the thread down the first and last sewing stations of the spine reinforces the structure of the exposed binding and allows it to effectively travel from the front cover to the back cover, or vice-versa. Draw the needle to the right of the next linking stitch and then pass it under the stitch in between the signatures and toward the top of the spine. Pull the thread taut. (F). Continue hiking down the top linking stitches of the spine by wrapping the thread once around each of the linking stitches (G) and pulling the thread taut each time until you reach the bottom signature (H).

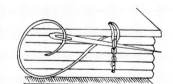

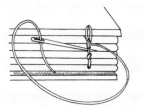

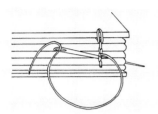

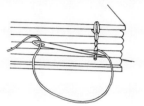

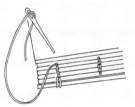

8. Attach the first (leftmost) hole of the back cover using the same double-loop method as above (I, J, K). Do not travel back up the spine with the thread. Instead, guide the needle into the nearest hole of the bottom signature and tie it off inside (see Tying Off the Binding, page 27).

9. Remove the needle from the end of the thread and thread it onto the remaining tail at the other end of the book. Repeat the method above to attach the cover holes at the right of the spine.

BINDING WITH AN EVEN NUMBER OF SIGNATURES

Bindings with an even number of signatures will have loose threads located at the same end of the spine and will require the extra step of drawing one of the threads to the other side of the spine before attaching the covers.

1. Choose one of the loose threads and attach a needle to it.

2. Enter the needle into the nearest sewing station of the nearest signature and pull the thread to the inside.

3. Draw the thread to the farthest sewing station at the end of the signature and exit, pulling the thread to the outside. Pull the thread taut.

Now you will have loose threads at each end of the spine. Continue to attach the covers as directed.

Tying Off the Binding

After you've completed sewing the signatures and the covers are attached (either one side or both), you'll need to tie off the binding to secure it.

1. Enter into the nearest signature (A) and pull the thread taut on the inside of the signature (B).

2. Guide the needle underneath the thread between the nearest sewing stations and make a true kettle stitch (page 24) (C, D). Repeat the stitch again (E, F), and then trim the thread to ¼ inch (6 mm) (G).

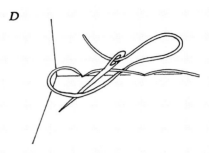

D

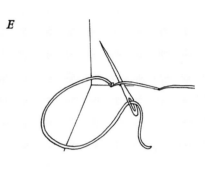

E

A

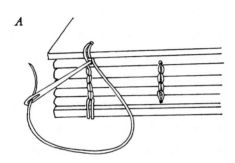

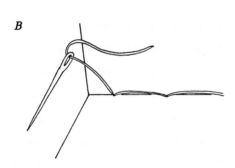

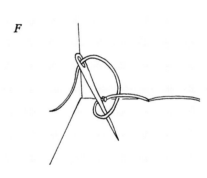

F

B

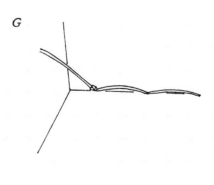

G

C

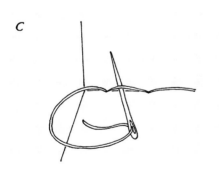

Other Knots and Stitches

Throughout the book, I will refer to the following knots and stitches that are best instructed through illustration.

Square Knot

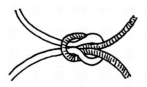

Lark's Head Knot

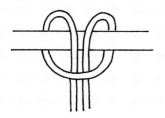

Overhand Stitch
(also called Whipstitch or Overcast Stitch)

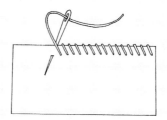

Loop Knot

CARING FOR YOUR BOOK

Always wrap your exposed-spine journal in a protective cover when traveling or carrying it in a bag. It can be as simple as wrapping the book in cloth or a piece of leather. This will protect the linen thread on the exposed binding from wear and tear.

Keep your book away from excess moisture such as rain or steam. Journaling while soaking in the bath may sound like a great idea, but it will likely compromise the structure of your journal. Moisture and steam can cause warping and waving of the cover boards and text block.

Rejuvenate your leather-covered book with a leather balm when the surface begins to look dry or worn.

Once your journal or book has lived a full and adventurous life, it might be time to meet its maker. Consider reusing the cover materials and replacing the text block with fresh pages. To do so, simply snip the thread and gently remove it from the binding, signatures, and cover. Then assemble a new text block and rebind the journal. (For more on disassembling old books, see page 19.)

TIPS FOR PACKAGING AND STORING YOUR BOOKS

Want to give your book as a gift or keep it safe for traveling or storage? Here are a few ideas.

For Packaging

Wrap the book you are giving in a vintage sewing pattern, piece of vintage cloth, embroidered handkerchief, or outdated newspaper. Include a library filing card with information about the materials used to make the book.

Make it more personal by including a typed (page 45) or handwritten dedication on the first page of the book.

For Storing or Display

1. Show off your hand-bound journals in an antique hatbox or a small suitcase.

2. Keep them safe by wrapping them in cloth and placing them in a lined cigar box.

3. Stack your journals between vintage books and use a book strap (page 131) to hold them together.

VINTAGE
BOOKS

LITTLE GOLDEN PICTURE BOOK

*Don't take the little things for granted. This Victorian–inspired
miniphoto book is to faint over . . . sigh . . . or just the perfect size
to hold the moments most dear to your heart.*

PREPARE THE COVER

1. Take apart the used book. (See Deconstructing a Vintage Hardcover, page 19.) You will only need one cover board for this project.

2. Turn the remaining cover over so the inside is facing up. Align the ruler inside one of the edges of the board where the lining paper overlaps the edge of the cloth. Use a craft knife to gently make a cut down the entire length of the board through the lining paper only.

3. Insert the blade inside the cut beneath the book cloth. Gently pull the edge of the cloth up and away from the board (A).

4. Pull the entire edge of cloth away from the board. Repeat for the remaining three edges.

5. Turn the board over and gently peel the entire cloth cover off the board and set it aside (B).

6. Use a paper cutter to cut the board into two smaller boards. Each should measure 4¾ x 3 inches (12 x 7.6 cm).

7. Use scissors to trim the folded edges off the cloth. Cut the cloth in half at the horizontal midline.

8. Position one of the cloth pieces back side up on your work surface. Place one of the 4¾ x 3-inch (12 x 7.6 cm) boards on the back of the cloth (C).

9. Use a ruler to measure ½ inch (1.3 cm) around the outer edges of the board. Mark this distance all the way around the outside of the board using a pencil and a metal ruler. Use scissors to cut away the cloth just outside the line (D). Repeat for the second board and cloth.

10. Place a piece of wax paper on your work surface and place one of the boards on top of it. Apply a thin coat of glue to the board. Center it, glue side down, onto the back of one of the cloths. Turn the cloth over and use a bone folder to smooth it out. Turn the cloth over so the board is facing up.

11. Measure ⅛ inch (3 mm) from each of the four outer corners of the cover boards and mark with a pencil. Position a ruler diagonally across each mark and draw a line (E).

12. Use scissors to trim off all four corners.

13. Use a brush to apply a thin layer of glue to the entire bottom edge of the cloth. Fold the glued edge of the cloth up to meet the back side of the board. Use a bone folder to smooth the edge, pressing the cloth onto the board. Repeat for the top edge. Repeat for the side edges.

14. Choose one of the gold sheets measuring 4½ x 2¾ inches (11.4 x 7 cm) and use a brush to apply a thin coat of glue to the back side of it.

finished dimensions

4¾ x 3 x 1 inches (12 x 7.6 x 2.5 cm)

stitches used

Coptic stitch (page 22), true kettle stitch (page 24)

what you need

Basic Bookmaking Toolkit (page 13)

Bookbinding thread, 56 inches (142 cm)

Used book cover, front cover at least 6 x 8 inches (15.2 x 20.3 cm)

2 sheets of gold paper, 4½ x 2¾ inches (11.4 x 7 cm)

28 sheets of 80 lb. black writing paper, 9 x 2¾ inches (22.9 x 7 cm)

21 strips of 80 lb. black writing paper, 1¼ x 2¾ inches (3.2 x 7 cm)

2 strips of gold paper, 1¼ x 2¾ inches (3.2 x 7 cm)

2 sheets of gold paper, 5 x 2¾ inches (12.7 x 7 cm)

1 sheet of cardstock, 3 x 2¾ inches (7.6 x 7 cm)

Gold button

24 inches (61 cm) of gold or black thread

60 Gold or black photo corners

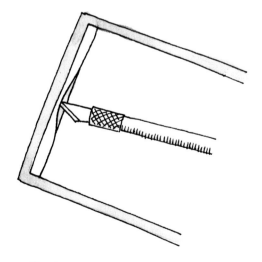

fig. A

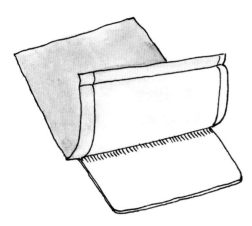

fig. B

fig. C

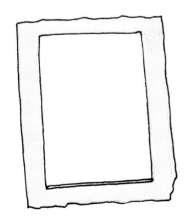

fig. D

15. Adhere the sheet, centered, onto the inner cover and use a bone folder to smooth it out. Repeat with the other gold sheet and the remaining cover board.

MAKE THE TEXT BLOCK

16. Divide the 9 x 2¾-inch (22.9 x 7 cm) black writing paper into stacks of four sheets each. With the bone folder, fold each stack into a signature measuring 4½ x 2¾ inches (11.4 x 7 cm). Arrange the signatures into a text block and set them aside.

17. Fold each of the 21 strips of black paper and 2 strips of gold paper in half vertically so they measure ⅝ x 2¾ inches (1.4 x 7 cm). These folded strips will act as spacers between the pages to accommodate the thickness of the photos (see figure F).

18. Set the top signature of the text block upright in front of you so that you are looking down onto the top edge of the pages. Partially fan it open and position the pages slightly apart from one another. Insert a black spacer along the spine between the first and second sheets. Place another one between the second and third sheets and another between the third and fourth sheets. Each signature will have a total of three black spacers. Place black spacers the same way within the remaining signatures (F).

19. Position the text block so the spine is facing you. Place a gold spacer on the outside spine of the third and fifth signatures.

20. Place the gold sheets measuring 5 x 2¾ inches (12.7 x 7 cm) on the top page of the first signature and the bottom page of the final signature with the fore edge, top, and bottom edges aligning, and the extra width wrapping around the spine edges. The text block should now have a spine with signatures alternating in color from gold to black (G).

PUNCH HOLES IN THE SIGNATURES

21. Use the sheet of cardstock to create a punch guide (page 17), using Template 1 as a guide.

22. Nest the punch template inside each signature (including the wraparound end sheets and spacers), place the signature in the gutter of a phonebook (page 15) and use an awl to punch all sewing stations. After each signature is punched, arrange them into a text block.

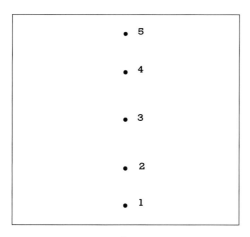

template 1
3 x 2¾ inches (7.6 x 7 cm)

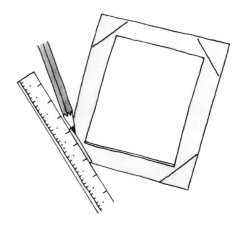

fig. E

PUNCH HOLES IN THE COVERS

23. Create a cover punch guide from cardstock using Template 2. Center the guide within the top and bottom edges of the front cover. With a pencil, mark the top, midpoint, and bottom sewing stations on the cover ¼ inch (6 mm) from the spine edge. Mark the two holes near the fore edge of the cover. Turn the guide over and repeat for the back cover. Use an awl to punch the marked holes on both covers. You will have a total of five holes on each cover board.

template 2
4¾ x 3 inches (12 x 7.6 cm)

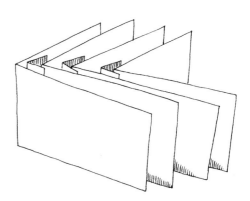

fig. F

fig. G

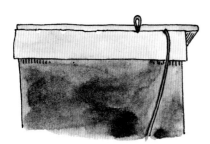

fig. H

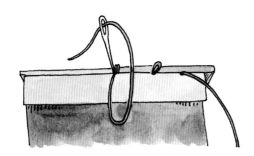

fig. I

fig. J

ASSEMBLE THE BOOK

24. Prepare the text block for binding. Make certain all pages are in order, including the end sheets and the alternating spacers. Place the text block inside the covers.

25. Begin binding signature 1: Draw the threaded needle into sewing station 1 and out through sewing station 2, leaving 8 inches (20.3 cm) of loose thread hanging outside the first station. Reenter through the second station and form a loop that will be used to link the following signature (H).

26. Draw the needle and thread out through the center sewing station (station 3) and loop it twice around the spine cover and through the center hole in the cover. Reenter stewing station 3 (I).

27. Draw the needle and thread out through sewing station 4 and, reenter through the same sewing station to form a loop that will be used to link the following signature.

28. Draw the needle out through the last sewing station (station 5).

29. Signature 2: Draw the needle into sewing station 5 and out through sewing station 4. At the fourth sewing station, put the needle and thread through the open loop and pull the threads taut.

30. Reenter through sewing station 4 and out through the center sewing station (3). Link the center sewing stations with a basic Coptic stitch and reenter that same sewing station.

31. In the next sewing station (station 2), again draw the thread through the loop to link the signatures. Pull the thread taut.

32. Reenter through the second sewing station and out through sewing station 1. Link the first and second signatures with a square knot (page 28).

33. Signatures 3 through 6: Continue with the basic Coptic stitch method with linking true kettle stitches at the top and bottom stations.

34. Signature 7: Continue with the basic Coptic stitch. At sewing station 3, link to the previous station 2, pull the thread taut, guide the needle between signatures 6 and 7, and then pull the thread taut.

35. Place the remaining cover on the text block and loop twice around the outside of the center hole.

36. Reenter into the center hole of the signature.

37. Continue sewing the signature and leave the thread long after the final kettle stitch (J).

38. Use the loose threads to attach the covers (see page 25). Tie off the loose threads in the inside of the nearest signature (see page 27).

ATTACH THE CLOSURE

39. Sew a button onto the top cover using gold or black thread.

40. Back cover: Using a needle threaded with 16 inches (40.6 cm) of gold thread, enter into the hole closest to the center of the book on the outside of the cover. Pull the thread into the inside of the cover and enter into the other hole (K).

41. Remove the needle and place it onto the other loose end of thread (L).

42. Guide the needle through the second hole.

43. Remove the needle. Pull both ends of the thread until they are even. Make a square knot with the thread on the outside of the cover's fore edge near the holes and leave the ends of the thread loose (M).

44. Fasten the cover by wrapping the loose ends of the thread around the button on the front cover.

45. To fill your Golden Picture Book, place photo corners on the corners of your photos, peel the backing from the corners, and stick them to the pages. Or, if the corners come on a roll, peel them from the roll first, and then place them on the photos' corners and stick the photos to the pages.

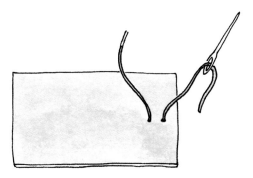

fig. K

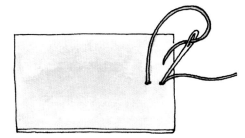

fig. L

fig. M

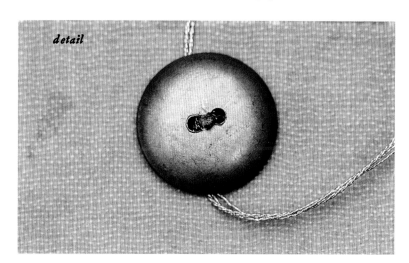

detail

BOOKMARK

Instead of throwing away the spine from the book you disassembled for Little Golden Picture Book (page 32), you can create a beautiful vintage bookmark.

1. Measure the spine.

2. Cut a strip from the decorative paper that matches the dimensions of the spine.

3. Cover your work surface with a piece of wax paper. Place the decorative paper on the wax paper with the back side facing up and apply a thin coat of glue to it.

4. Adhere the back of the spine piece to the glued side of the decorative paper. Use a bone folder to smooth any air bubbles.

5. Use scissors to trim any extra decorative paper that overhangs the edges of the spine piece, if needed.

6. Use a ruler and pencil to locate and mark a point ¼ inch (6 mm) from the top edge of the spine and at the midpoint between the side edges. Use a hole punch to punch through the point (A).

7. Thread the needle with all three pieces of embroidery floss.

8. Guide the needle and floss through the hole in the spine from front to back until the floss is an even length on both sides (B, C). Remove the needle and set it aside.

9. Gather all ends of the threads in one hand and pull to align the ends if necessary. The center of the threads should be positioned at the hole in the spine.

10. Form a single loose loop knot (page 28) near the top edge of the spine (D). Tighten the knot by pushing it firmly toward the edge of the spine. Pull thread ends to lock the knot.

11. Trim the thread ends 1½ inches (3.8 cm) from the knot.

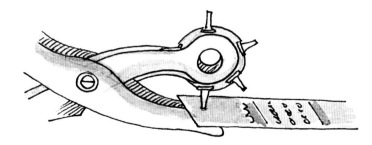

fig. A

stitches used

Loop knot (page 28)

what you need

Basic Bookmaking Toolkit (page 13)

Cloth spine from a vintage book, about 1 x 6 inches (2.5 x 15.2 cm)

Decorative paper, at least 2 x 8 inches (5.1 x 20.3 cm)

¹⁄₃₂-inch (0.8 mm) hole punch

Large-eye embroidery needle

Three 10-inch (25.4 cm) lengths of embroidery floss

fig. B

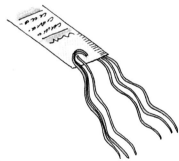

fig. C

fig. D

PRESERVE-A-MEMORY MASON-JAR BOOK

Yes, the Rainier cherries you canned were delicious, but what about the summer afternoon you and your sweetheart handpicked them from the orchard? Preserve it: the romance, the weather, and the sweet (or sour) disposition of the day.

FOLD THE SIGNATURES

1. Divide the text-weight paper into stacks of five sheets. Fold each stack into signatures that measure 1⅛ x 4½ inches (2.9 x 11.4 cm). You will have 18 signatures total.

OPTIONAL:

• Before folding, randomly replace 10 of the plain sheets of paper with the optional decorative fruit-print sheets.

• Round all four corners of each folded signature with a corner rounder.

PUNCH THE HOLES

2. Create the punch guide from cardstock (page 17) using Template 1. Nest the template within each signature and punch the holes with the awl.

ASSEMBLE THE BOOK

3. Align the punched signatures in the order you would like them to appear.

4. Beginning with the top signature, enter the single-threaded needle into sewing station 1 and sew the text block together using the running stitch binding method with French stitches between stations 2 and 3, and between stations 6 and 7. Link the top and bottom stations together with a true kettle stitch. Sewing stations 4 and 5 will sew over the ribbon using the "sewing over tapes" method (page 20). Be sure to leave 8 inches (20.3 cm) of loose ribbon at the beginning of the first signature and at the end of the last signature (A).

5. Gently pull one end of the ribbon to center the tail ends evenly on each side of the spine.

6. Finish by knotting the thread tails inside the nearest signature (page 27), and trim them to ¼ inch (6 mm).

LABEL THE JAR

7. With a drafting compass, draw a 2¼-inch (5.7 cm) circle on the adhesive paper. Cut out the circle and adhere it to the top of the lid or on the glass surface of the jar. Label it with the date and/or title of your book.

NOTE: The text block may be stored in the jar with the pages fanned open in a cylinder shape, or as a conventional rectangular text block with the pages fastened with the ribbon. If it's fanned open, the ribbon serves the purpose of lifting the book out of the jar.

• 8

• 7

• 6

• 5

• 4

• 3

• 2

• 1

template 1
2 x 4½ inches
(enlarge template by 25%)

finished dimensions

1¼ x 4½ x 1½ inches (3.1 x 11.4 x 3.8 cm)

stitches used

Running stitch (page 20), French stitch (page 24), long stitch (page 21)

what you need

Basic Bookmaking Toolkit (page 13)

Bookbinding thread, 95 inches (241 cm)

90 sheets of text-weight paper, 4½ x 2¼ inches (11.4 x 5.7 cm)

Decorative fruit-printed paper, cut into ten 4½ x 2¼-inch (11.4 x 5.7 cm) rectangles (optional)

Corner rounder (optional)

1 sheet of cardstock, 8½ x 11 inches (21.6 x 27.9 cm)

15 inches (38.1 cm) of ribbon or cloth tape, ½ inch (1.3 cm) wide

Drafting compass

1 sheet of adhesive label paper

1 wide-mouth 1-pint (473 ml) canning jar

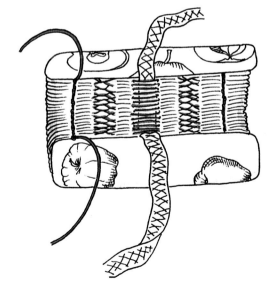

fig. A

IN MEMORIAM

My great grandma was a stunner, and a trio of wily gents chased her hand. Uncle Benny was a rodeo clown who dodged raging bulls. Preserve your family stories—and who chased whom—in this heirloom memoir book.

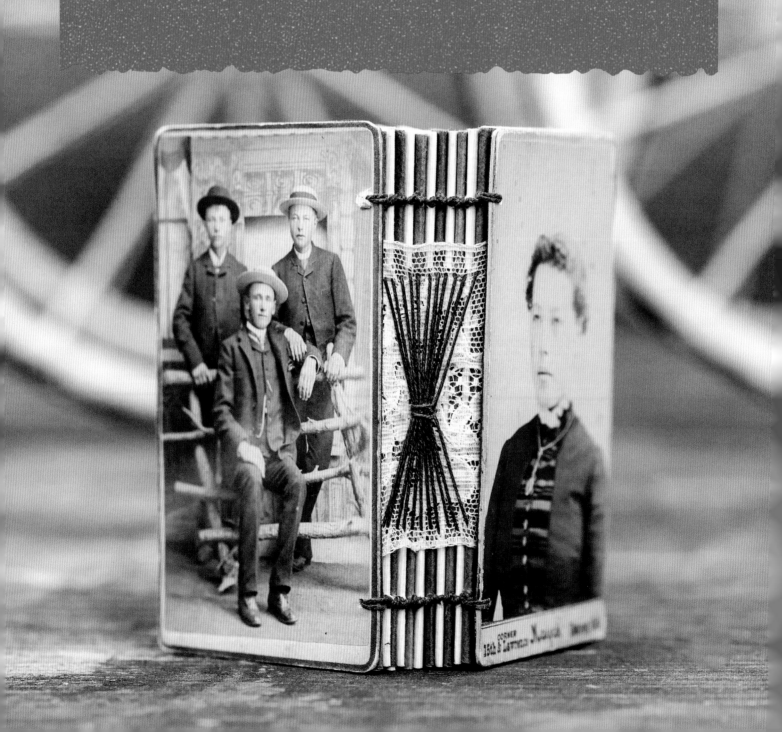

MAKE THE SIGNATURES

1. To determine the dimensions of the pages, measure the height and width of one of the vintage photo cards. Subtract ¼ inch (3 mm) from the height. Multiply the width by two, then subtract ¼ inch (6 mm). Cut 44 sheets of writing paper to the size you calculated.

2. Separate the paper into 11 stacks of four sheets each. Jog each stack and fold in half to make a signature, creasing with the bone folder. There will be 11 total signatures. Using the corner rounder, round the outer corners of each folded signature, if you want to.

   OPTIONAL: You can add a dedication or a message to the first page of any journal before you bind it together. (See page 45.)

MAKE END SHEETS AND SPACERS FOR THE SIGNATURES

3. The end sheets and spacers are both constructed from lokta paper. For the end sheets, cut two pieces of paper the same height as your signatures and the same width as your signature plus ⅜ inch (9.5 mm). Wrap each of these pieces around the front and back signatures, lining one edge of the end sheet to the fore edge of the signature and wrapping the remaining length around the fold of the signature. Half of the sheet can be used for spaces while the other half for endpapers. (See B, page 104.)

4. The spacers will cover alternating signatures so only four are needed. Cut four strips of the lokta paper the same height as the signatures and ¾ inch (1.9 cm) wide. Wrap each strip around the folded edges of four signatures. Arrange the signatures so the brown and white folded edges alternate and create a striped pattern (A).

MAKE A GUIDE AND PUNCH HOLES IN THE SIGNATURES

5. Create a guide for punching four holes in each signature (see page 17). Take a center sheet from one of the signature to use as a guide, and cut the cardstock to match the height and width of the entire spread. Return the sheet to the interior of the signature. Next measure ½ inch (1.3 cm) and 1 inch (2.5 cm) from both the top and bottom of the folded edge and mark on the fold line. Use the awl to punch holes through the four measured marks.

6. Nest the punch guide you made within a signature, making certain the edges are aligned. Place the signature and the guide in the gutter of an open phonebook, holding them securely in alignment. Gently push the awl through all four stations (B). Repeat for each signature.

finished dimensions

2½ x 4 x 1 inches (6.4 x 10.2 x 2.5 cm)

stitches used

True kettle stitch (page 24), with running stitch variation (page 20), gathering stitch (page 24)

what you need

Basic Bookmaking Toolkit (page 13)

Bookbinding thread, 70 inches (178 cm)

2 vintage photo cards, approximately 2½ x 4 inches (6.4 cm x 10.2 cm), at least ⅟₂₅ inch (1 mm) thick

24 sheets of acid-free writing paper, 8½ x 11 inches (21.6 x 27.9 cm)

Corner rounder (optional)

1 sheet of brown lokta paper, 8½ x11 inches (21.6 x 27.9 cm)

1 sheet of velvet decorative paper, 6 x 5 inches (15.2 x 12.7 cm)

Ribbon or lace, approximately 6 inches long and 2½ inches (6.4 cm) wide or less (optional)

fig. A

fig. B

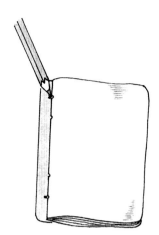

fig. C

PREPARE THE COVERS

7. To cover the back sides of the photographs with the velvet decorative paper, first coat the back of the photo card with a thin layer of glue using a glue brush. Press the coated card to the back side of the chosen paper or cloth. Use a bone folder to carefully smooth out any air bubbles. Let the glue dry for a few minutes. Closely trim the overhanging edges with scissors.

8. Punch two holes in each photo card cover. The holes will be used to attach the boards to the text block. To find the location of the holes, center the text block inside the covers and use a pencil to mark a hole ⅛ inch (3 mm) from the outside edge of the board in each end of the covers to line up with the top and bottom sewing stations (C). Place the covers faceup on a cutting mat and use the awl to punch the holes. Make the holes large enough to allow the single-threaded needle head to pass through twice.

ASSEMBLE THE BOOK

9. Sew the text block together using the running stitch binding method with true kettle stitches to link the top and bottom sewing stations of each signature together. Be sure to leave at least 8 inches (20.3 cm) of loose thread at the first and last sewing stations so that it may be used to attach the covers.

NOTE: For the optional lace accent, securely hold the lace in place with your hand and sew directly through the holes for the entire binding (D). If the lace is narrower than the space between the middle sewing stations, sew over rather than through it. After completing the binding, trim the lace to align with the inner fore edges of the cover boards and provide a textural accent within the covers of the book.

10. On the final signature, exit from the second sewing station. Make a gathering stitch (page 24) using the threads from all of the previous signatures. From there, continue into the third sewing station and complete the binding with a true kettle stitch at the end station. Leave the remaining thread for attaching the covers (E).

11. Attach the covers (see Attaching the Covers, page 25).

fig. D

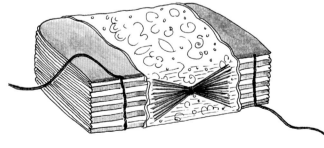

fig. E

ADD TYPE

Personalize your book with a title or dedicate it to the memory of your ancestor or loved one.

1. Before sewing your text block, remove the outside sheet from signature 1. The outer right page will be the page you will type on. I will refer to it as page 1.

2. Measure the dimensions of page 1 with a ruler. Use scissors to cut out the same size page from the sheet of writing paper. This will be your practice sheet.

3. Decide what you would like to type. If you would like it centered on the page, use a ruler to locate the center of the sheet and mark it with a pencil on the practice sheet.

4. Insert the practice sheet into the typewriter. Practice typing out your title or dedication until you are satisfied.

5. Insert page 1 into your typewriter (either with the signature open or closed) and type your final title or dedication.

6. Return page 1 to the outside of the first signature and continue binding as instructed.

what you need

Page 1 of your journal

Ruler

Scissors

1 sheet of scrap paper, 8½ x 11 inches (21.6 x 27.9 cm)

Pencil

Typewriter

REINCARNATE JOURNAL

I believe books deserve more than one life, especially beautifully crafted ones that are falling apart and in need of a little—or a lot—of care. Claim what is remaining and revive it with this homespun curative.

PREPARE THE COVER

1. Carefully deconstruct the used book (page 19).

2. Since you'll be using the book's spine as tapes in the binding, you'll need it to be a little more rigid. To add strength to it, measure its dimensions and cut a matching piece of paper from the decorative sheet. Glue the decorative paper to the back of the spine. Flatten any bubbles with a bone folder and set it aside to dry. After a few minutes, use a pair of scissors to make a horizontal cut at the midpoint, cutting the spine in half. The two resulting pieces will be your tapes for sewing over in the binding.

3. To prepare the cover boards, apply glue to the raw spine edges of each board using a glue brush. Fold the raw edges over the spine and press them to the back side of the boards. Continue to apply pressure with your fingertips until the edges adhere to the board. You may also place wax paper on the backs of the boards and set them inside a book press or stack weights on top of them for a few minutes while they dry.

4. Prepare the decorative paper that will cover the inside of the cover boards. It will be the same dimension as your folded signatures (see step 7).

5. Measure and cut the sheets to size. Lay one backing paper facedown on a piece of wax paper. With a brush, apply a thin coat of glue to the backside paper. Adhere the glued paper to the inside of one cover and smooth any bubbles with a bone folder. Repeat for the remaining cover. Set them aside to dry for a few minutes.

MAKE THE TEXT BLOCK

6. Divide the text-weight paper into stacks of five sheets each. With your bone folder, fold each stack into signatures measuring 5½ x 8½ inches (14 x 21.6 cm).

7. Use the following instructions to determine the final dimension of the signatures: Measure the width of the front cover and subtract ⅛ inch (3 mm); this is the final width of the signatures. Measure the height of the front cover and subtract ¼ inch (6 mm); this is the final height of the signatures. Use a paper cutter to cut all signatures to the final size.

finished dimensions

Depends upon size of the recycled cover

stitches used

Running stitch (page 20), Coptic stitch (page 22), true kettle stitch (page 24), sewing over tapes stitch (page 18)

what you need

Basic Bookmaking Toolkit (page 13)

Used book, 5½ x 8½-inch (14 x 21.6 cm) maximum size

Book press or weights (optional)

4 sheets of decorative paper, 8½ x 11 inches (21.6 x 27.9 cm)

55 sheets of text-weight paper, 11 x 8½ inches (27.9 x 21.6 cm)

1 sheet of cardstock, 5½ x 8½ inches (14 x 21.6 cm)

fig. A

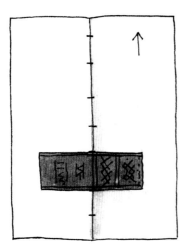

fig. B

8. Determine the dimensions of the end sheets. They will be the same height as the signature by the width of the signature plus ¾ inch (1.9 cm).

9. Cut two end sheets out of the decorative paper with the paper cutter. Place the end sheets on the top page of the first signature and the back page of the final signature, with the extra width wrapping around the spine edges of the signatures. (See figure B, page 104.) Do not glue them.

10. Determine the dimensions of the four decorative spacers that wrap around alternating spine edges on the signatures. They will be the same height as the signature and 1½ inches (3.8 cm) wide.

11. Cut four spacers from the decorative paper and fold each in half so they're ¾ inch (1.9 cm) wide. Wrap the spacers around the spine edge of the third, fifth, seventh, and ninth signatures so the spine of the text block appears striped (A). Do not glue them.

CREATE A PUNCH GUIDE

12. To make a punch guide, first determine its dimensions. It will be the same height as the signature and 5 inches (12.7 cm) wide. Cut the template from a sheet of cardstock to the determined size. Make a vertical fold in the template at the midpoint, folding it in half lengthwise. Smooth the fold with your bone folder.

13. Open the template and place it on your work surface. Measure 1 inch (2.5 cm) from the top and bottom of the guide and use a pencil to mark the points along the fold. Determine the midpoint of the guide and mark it along the fold. Draw an arrow on the inside of the guide to signify the upright position.

14. Center one of the tapes (from step 2) horizontally between the top point and the midpoint. With a pencil, mark both the top and bottom edges of the tape along the fold of the guide. Center the second tape horizontally between the midpoint and the bottom point. Mark both edges of the tape along the fold again. You will have a total of seven marks on the guide (B). These will be your sewing stations.

PUNCH HOLES IN THE SIGNATURES

15. Nest the punch guide upright inside each signature (including the wrap-around end sheets and spacers) and use an awl to punch all seven sewing stations. After each signature is punched, arrange them into a text block.

TIP: To punch holes in the spacers, temporarily nest a spacer between the interior of the signature and the punch guide. This will hold the spacer in place. Return the spacer to the outside of the signature when you're finished.

PUNCH HOLES IN THE COVERS

16. Fold the punch guide and align it in the upright position to the spine of the cover board. Center the guide within the top and bottom edges of the cover. With a pencil, mark the top, middle, and bottom sewing stations on the cover ¼ inch (6 mm) from the spine edge (C). Repeat for the back cover.

17. Using an awl, punch the marked holes in both covers. You will have a total of six holes.

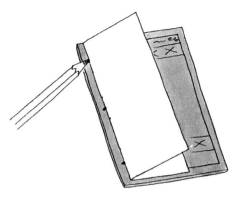

fig. C

PREPARE THE THREAD

18. Multiply the height of the front cover by 13. This is the number of inches of thread you will need. Measure and cut this amount from your spool. If the thread is unwaxed, run it over a bar of beeswax.

ASSEMBLE THE BOOK

19. Prepare the text block for binding. Make certain all pages are in order, including the end sheets and the alternating spacers. Place the text block inside the covers. Place the book front side up, with the top and bottom tapes near the section of the spine each will be sewn to either side of the center (D).

20. Gently pull the bottom signature from the unbound book. Beginning with this signature, enter into sewing station 1 (the bottom hole) from the outside and pull the thread to the inside of the signature. Leave 8 inches (20.3 cm) of loose thread on the outside of the signature.

21. Enter into sewing station 2 and pull the thread to the outside of the signature. Position one of the two tapes you made from the used book's spine between stations 2 and 3.

22. Pull the thread around the outside of the tape and enter into sewing station 3. Pull the thread to the inside of the signature and tighten it around the tape to hold it in place.

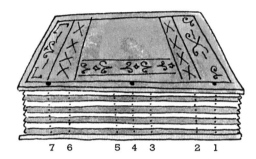

fig. D

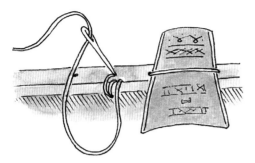

fig. E

fig. F

23. Enter through sewing station 4 and pull the thread to the outside of the signature. Place the bottom cover beneath the signature and align the center holes. Pull the thread to the outside of the cover and enter into the center hole. Pull the thread through the cover hole. Again, pull the thread to the outside of the cover and enter into the center hole of the cover, forming a double wrap around the spine of the cover. Pull the thread to the outside of the signature and enter into sewing station 4 (E). Pull the thread to the inside of the signature.

24. Enter through sewing station 5 and pull the thread to the outside of the signature. Position the other tape between sewing stations 5 and 6. Pull the thread around the outside of the tape and enter into sewing station 6. Pull the thread to the inside of the signature and tighten it around the tape to hold it in place.

25. Enter into sewing station 7 and pull the thread to the outside of the signature.

26. Pull the next signature from the unbound text block, place it on top of the bottom signature and enter into sewing station 7 (the nearest hole).

27. Continue binding the book using the same directions as above, altered with the following: signatures 2 through 10 will make a Coptic stitch at sewing station 4 rather than linking to the cover. Link all signatures at the end sewing stations with a true kettle stitch. Once you reach the top signature, make a Coptic stitch link to the previous signature, and then wrap around the cover at sewing station 4 in the same manner as in step 23.

OPTIONAL: You may also choose to gather the threads over the tapes (page 44, Step 10). Leave the thread long after the final kettle stitch. It will be used in the final step to attach the covers.

28. When the binding of the text block is complete, center each tape by gently rocking them beneath the threads so an equal amount of the tape hangs off both edges. Gently fold the edges of the tapes beneath the cover boards (F).

29. Use the loose threads to attach the covers (see Attaching the Covers, page 25).

CIGAR BOX BOOKS

The pampered lifestyle of kings and queens is lost to most of us, but you can re-create it with hand-sewn books. This set of mini journals may strike your fancy or serve as an honorable gift to the royal persona in your life.

finished dimensions

Depends upon the original box size

stitches used

Coptic stitch (page 22), running stitch (page 20), gathering stitch (page 24)

what you need

Basic Bookmaking Toolkit (page 13)

Cardboard cigar box

Fine sandpaper

Paintbrush

Black India ink

2 sheets of decorative paper, 8½ x 11 inches (21.6 x 27.9 cm)

25 sheets of text-weight paper, 8½ x 11 inches (21.6 x 27.9 cm)

1 sheet of cardstock, 8½ x 11 inches (21.6 x 27.9 cm)

fig. A

MAKE THE COVERS

1. Cut the lid off the cardboard cigar box by gently running a craft knife along the inside hinge of the top panel and repeating until all layers of the cardboard are cut. Working from the inside of the cardboard cigar box, gently cut through the layers of board at all side joints (where the side panels meet each other in the corners). Cut the remaining joints that link the side panels to the bottom panel of the box. Once that's done, you will have six individual boards.

2. With a paper cutter, even out the raw edges of the boards so they're straight.

3. Smooth the cut edges of the boards by lightly sanding them with fine sandpaper. Depending upon the age of your cigar box, some of the printed label paper may flake off. This is okay—it adds to the vintage look.

4. Cover your worktable with wax or craft paper to protect it from the ink. With a brush and undiluted India ink, paint the raw edges of the boards with one or two coats. Allow the edges to dry completely.

5. When they're dry, pair the boards according to size. There will be three pairs total (A).

6. Choose any cover board. With a glue brush and glue, coat the back side of the board with a thin layer of glue.

7. Position the glued side of the board on the back of one decorative paper sheet.

8. Press the paper to the board and smooth out any air bubbles with the bone folder.

9. Use the scissors or craft knife to cut the extra decorative paper edges from the glued board (B).

10. Repeat these steps for each remaining cover board.

MAKE THE SIGNATURES

11. To determine the dimensions of the pages for the journals, choose one of the cover boards and measure it. Write this measurement on a piece of scratch paper. Subtract ¼ inch (6 mm) from the height. Multiply the width of the cover board side by two, and then subtract ¼ inch (6 mm) from that total. For example, your paper size would be 7¾ x 4¾ inches (19.7 x 12 cm) if you had 4 x 5-inch (10.2 x 12.7 cm) covers.

12. With your paper cutter, cut 45 sheets of text-weight paper to this size. Separate the sheets into nine piles of five each. (There will be nine signatures in each journal.)

13. Use the bone folder to fold each stack into a signature.

14. Repeat steps 11 through 13 for each remaining set of covers.

CREATE A PUNCH GUIDE

15. Determine the dimensions of the guide—it will be the same height as your signature and 2 inches (5.1 cm) wide. Cut the template from the sheet of cardstock to the determined size. Fold the template in half lengthwise, so it's the same height as before and 1 inch (2.5 cm) wide. Smooth the crease with your bone folder.

16. Open the template and place it on your work surface.

17. Measure ½ inch (1.3 cm) from the top and bottom of the guide, and mark these points along the inside of the fold line.

18. Measure 1 inch (2.5 cm) from the top and bottom of the guide and mark these points along the inside of the fold line as well. You will have a total of four marks on the fold. Draw an arrow on the inside of the guide to signify the upright position (C).

TIP: If your covers are more than 6 inches (15.2 cm) tall, you might consider adding more sewing stations in the center of the spine and as shown in the photo on page 51.

PUNCH THE HOLES IN THE SIGNATURES

19. Nest the punch guides inside the corresponding signatures in the gutter of a phonebook and punch holes with your awl where you made marks. Repeat for each set of signatures. After completing each set of signatures, stack them and place them within their matching covers.

fig. B

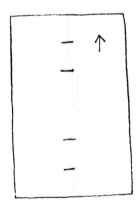

fig. C

fig. D

PUNCH THE HOLES IN THE COVER BOARDS

20. Choose a book set to start with. Remove the top cover and the top signature. Place them on your work surface with the cover board on top of the signature and the spines facing you.

21. Center the signature under the cover board so there's ⅛ inch (3 mm) of space at the top and bottom.

22. Slide the cover board back ¼ inch (6 mm) or so to reveal the spine of the signature underneath it so you can use its holes as a guide.

23. Mark the placement of the holes on the cover board using a pencil. They should correspond to the top and bottom sewing stations on the signature. The two marks should be placed ¼ inch (6 mm) from the spine edge of the board (D).

24. Use an awl to punch holes through the two marks.

25. Repeat steps 20 through 24 for the bottom board and all remaining cover boards.

ASSEMBLE THE BOOK

26. Align the signatures within the two covers of one book, and place it on your work surface.

27. Determine the length of the binding thread by measuring the height of the signature. Multiply the height of the spine by nine and add 24 inches (61 cm). This is the amount of thread needed to sew each book.

28. Pull the bottom signature from the stack. Enter a threaded needle into the outside of the rightmost sewing station and pull it into the center of the signature. Pull the needle until there is a 12-inch (30.5 cm) tail of thread remaining on the outside of the signature. Enter the thread into the second sewing station and pull it to the outside of the signature. Continue sewing in running stitch with true kettle stitches linking the signatures at the top and bottom sewing stations.

VARIATION: When you reach the final signature, you may wish to make a gathering stitch by looping around the previous running stitch threads. Complete the binding by linking the final sewing station to the previous signature with a true kettle stitch. Leave the thread long after the final stitch. It will be used to attach the covers.

29. Use the loose tail threads to attach the covers (page 25). Tie off the loose threads in the inside of the nearest signature and trim the tails to ¼ inch (6 mm). (See page 27.)

30. Repeat steps 24 through 29 for each journal set.

EXPOSED SPINE ALTERNATIVE

Tell your story, or at least hint at it, by adding decorative spacers to any exposed spine journal.

what you need

Basic Bookmaking Toolkit (page 13)

At least 5 signatures, punched and ready to be sewn with your choice of stitching

1 decorative paper or image, at least 9 x 4 inches

Prepare a text block that will be bound with an exposed spine. Follow the instructions given for your specific project. The text block should be one that has at least four sewing stations along the spine. Once the signatures are punched, complete the following steps:

1. Measure the distance between the two centermost stations and add ½ inch (1.3 cm) to that measurement.

MAKE AND PLACE THE SPACERS

2. Trim the decorative paper or image to the height of the measurement from step 1.

3. Cut the image into nine pieces that are 1 inch (2.5 cm) wide by the height from step 2. These will be the wraparound spacers you will add to decorate the spines of the signatures.

4. Fold each piece of decorative paper in half vertically, creasing them with the bone folder (A).

5. Nest all of the folded spacers together and gently jog them so the bottom and top edges and the center creases are aligned.

6. Pull one of the signatures from your text block. Position the stack of nested spacers along the outside spine of the signature. Adjust it so the spacers are centered over the middle sewing stations. The spacers should extend ¼ inch (6 mm) from the outside edge of both sewing stations. Hold the spacers firmly to the spine of the signature.

7. Open the signature (still holding the spacers in their centered position on the outside) and use an awl to carefully punch through the center holes, piercing from the inside of the signature and out through the spacers (B). Once the two center holes are punched through the nested stack of spacers, set the awl aside and return the signature to the stack.

8. Arrange all nine signatures so the spines are facing up. To do this, slightly open each of the signatures and prop both fore edges of the signature on your work surface.

9. Separate the spacers from their nested stack and position them on the spines of the signatures so each signature has one spacer wrapped around its spine. Align the holes of the spacers to the holes of the center stations on the signatures (C).

10. Carefully close each of the signatures while keeping the wraparound spacer intact. Arrange the signatures in the order they will be sewn in.

11. Return to the next step in your project and sew the text block as directed. Be sure to sew through the holes in each spacer, too!

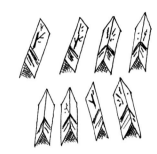

fig. A

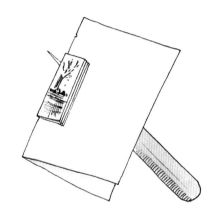

fig. B

fig. C

THE TAILOR'S DAUGHTER

*For some, a needle is a better ally than a pen.
This book is for writers who speak with lines of silk
and wool and paint the hills with daisy stitches.*

PREPARE THE COVER

1. Carefully take apart the used book. (See Deconstructing a Vintage Hardcover, page 19.) Set aside the spine piece to use later. You only need one of the two cover boards.

2. Turn the cover board over so the inside is facing up. Align the ruler inside one of the edges of the board where the lining paper overlaps the edge of the cloth. Use a craft knife to gently make a cut the entire length of the board through the paper. Insert the blade inside the cut beneath the book cloth (A).

3. Gently pull the entire edge of the cloth up and away from the board. Repeat for the remaining three edges. Turn the board over and gently peel the entire cloth cover off the board and set it aside.

4. Use a paper cutter to cut the board into two smaller boards measuring 4 x 5½ inches (10.2 x 14 cm).

5. Use scissors to trim the folded edges off the cloth. Fold the cloth in half to measure about 5 x 7 inches (12.7 x 17.8 cm). Cut the cloth in half along the horizontal midline.

6. Decorate the front cover cloth by freehand stitching with a threaded needle or a sewing machine.

7. Place a piece of wax paper on your work surface. Apply a thin coat of glue to one of the boards. Center the board, glue side down, onto the back of one of the cloths. Turn the board over and use a bone folder to smooth. Turn the cover over so the board is facing up again. Measure ⅛ inch (3 mm) from the four outer corners of the cover boards and mark with a pencil. Position a ruler diagonally across each mark and draw a line (B).

8. Use scissors to trim the marks along all four corners, snipping off the corners. Repeat for the remaining board and cloth.

finished dimensions

4 x 5½ x 1¼ inches (10.2 x 14 x 3.2 cm)

stitches used

Running stitch (page 20), true kettle stitch (page 24), Coptic stitch (page 22)

what you need

Basic Bookmaking Toolkit (page 13)

Bookbinding Thread, 56 inches (142 cm)

Used book with cover dimensions of at least 6 x 9½ inches (15.2 x 24.1 cm) and spine at least 1½ x 7 inches (3.8 x 17.8 cm)

Assorted threads and hand-sewing needle or sewing machine for decorating the cover and spine tabs

2 pieces of light- to medium-weight non-elastic decorative cloth, 4 x 5⅛ inches (10.2 x 13 cm) each

20 sheets of writing paper, 7½ x 5⅛ inches (19 x 13 cm)

10 pieces of mixed non-elastic cloth (burlap, cross-stitch, canvas, ticking), 7½ x 5⅛ inches (19 x 13 cm)

5 strips of cardstock, 1½ x 5⅛ inches (3.8 x 13 cm) each

5 strips of light- to medium-weight non-elastic decorative cloth, 2 x 5⅛ inches (5.1 x 13 cm) each

1 sheet of cardstock

Button

Button thread, 24 inches (61 cm)

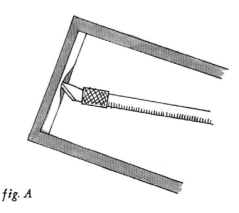

fig. A

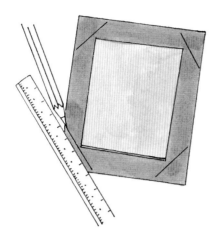

fig. B

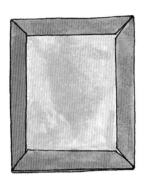

fig. C

fig. D

fig. E

9. Use a brush to apply a thin layer of glue to the entire bottom edge of the cloth. Fold the glued edge of the cloth up to meet the backside of the board. Use a bone folder to smooth the edge, pressing the cloth onto the board. Repeat for the top edge. Repeat for the side edges (C). Repeat steps 7 to 9 for the remaining board. Set aside.

10. Place the spine piece on your work surface. The spine will be turned into two tapes, so it will need to be flexible enough to bend at a right angle. If the spine piece is thin or brittle, apply a thin layer of glue to the back and adhere it to a piece of cardstock using your bone folder. Cut the extra cardstock from around the spine piece. Cut the spine piece into two pieces measuring 3½ x 1¼ inches (8.9 x 3.2 cm) (D). Decorate them by freehand stitching or use a sewing machine. Set aside.

11. Choose one of the decorative cloths measuring 4 x 5⅛ inches (10.2 x 13 cm) and use a brush to apply a thin coat of glue to the back side. Adhere the sheet to the inside cover and use a bone folder to smooth. Repeat for the other decorative sheet and cover board.

ASSEMBLE THE TEXT BLOCK

12. Divide the writing paper into stacks of four sheets. With your bone folder, fold each stack into a signature of 3¾ x 5⅛ inches (11.4 x 13 cm). Arrange the signatures into a text block.

13. Arrange the pieces of mixed cloth into groups of two. (I chose fabric with frayed edges to add some interest and texture.) Choose one group and place the two pieces of cloth in front of you horizontally and align all edges as closely as possible. Pull a signature from the text block and place it on the top cloth so the right edges of cloth and paper are aligned (E).

14. Fold the left edge of the cloth over the top of the paper signature. Smooth all layers of the signature and set aside. Repeat this step for all groups of cloth and the other four signatures. Arrange the new signatures into a text block.

15. Place a sheet of wax paper on your work surface and set one of the strips of cardstock on it. Apply a thin coat of glue to one side. Place one of the strips of decorative cloth back side up. Adhere the glued side of the paper strip to the back of the cloth. Use a bone folder to smooth. Use scissors to cut away the extra cloth. Repeat for the remaining strips of paper and cloth. These strips are the spacers that will wrap around the spine of the five signatures.

16. Place one of the completed spacers, back side up, on your work surface. Pull one of the signatures from the text block and align the spine edge to the vertical midline of the spacer. Wrap the spacer around the spine of the signature and use a bone folder to crease the spacer as best as possible. Repeat for the remaining spacers and signatures. Again arrange the signatures into a text block.

PUNCH HOLES IN THE SIGNATURES

17. Use the sheet of cardstock to create a template (see page 17) from Template 1.

18. Nest the punch template inside each signature (including the wrap-around spacers) and use an awl to punch all sewing stations. After each signature is punched, arrange them into a text block.

PUNCH HOLES IN THE COVERS

19. Fold the signature punch guide and align it with the spine of the cover board. Center the guide within the top and bottom edges of the cover. With a pencil, mark only the top, midpoint, and bottom sewing stations on the cover ¼ inch (6 mm) from the spine edge (F). Repeat for the back cover.

20. Using an awl, punch the marked holes on both covers. You will have a total of six holes, three on each cover.

ASSEMBLE THE BOOK

21. Prepare the text block for binding. Make certain all pages, including the spacers, are in order. Place the text block inside the covers. Orient the book front side up. Be sure to have the tapes you made from the original book's spine (step 10) nearby.

22. Gently pull the bottom signature from the unbound book. Beginning with this signature, enter into sewing station 1 and pull the thread to the inside of the signature. Leave 8 inches (20.3 cm) of loose thread on the outside of the signature.

23. Enter into station 2 and pull the thread to the outside of the signature. Position the first tape between stations 2 and 3.

24. Pull the thread around the outside of the tape and enter into station 3. Pull the thread to the inside of the signature and tighten it around the tape to hold it in place.

25. Enter through station 4 and pull the thread to the outside of the signature.

26. Place the bottom cover beneath the signature and align the center holes. Pull the thread to the outside of the cover and enter into the center hole. Pull the thread through the cover hole and toward the spine of the signature. Again, pull the thread to the outside of the cover and enter into the center hole of the cover, forming a doublewrap around the spine of the cover.

27. Pull the thread to the outside of the signature and reenter into station 4 (G). Pull the thread to the inside of the signature.

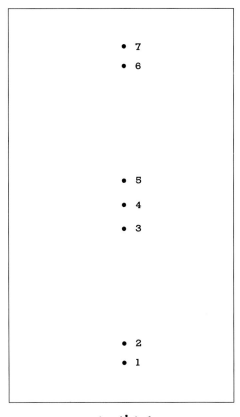

template 1
2 x 4½ inches

Enlarge template by 20%

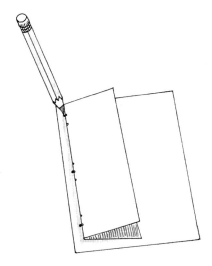

fig. F

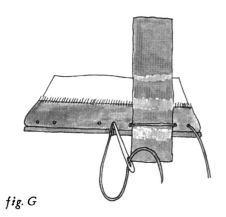

fig. G

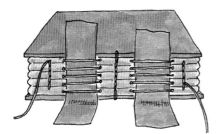

fig. H

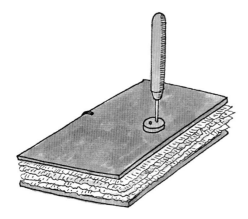

fig. I

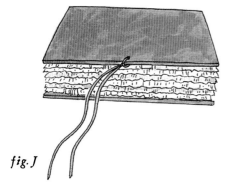

fig. J

28. Enter through station 5 and pull the thread to the outside of the signature. Position the remaining tape between stations 5 and 6. Pull the thread around the outside of the tape and enter into station 6. Pull the thread to the inside of the signature and tighten it around the tape to hold it in place.

29. Enter into station 7 and pull the thread outside the signature.

30. Pull the next signature from the unbound book, place it on top of the bottom signature and enter into station 7 (the nearest hole).

31. Continue binding the book using the same directions as above, with the following changes: Signatures 2 through 4 will make a Coptic stitch at station 4, rather than linking to the cover. Link all signatures at the top and bottom stations with a true kettle stitch. Once you reach the final (top) signature, make a Coptic stitch link to the previous signature at station 4, then guide the needle underneath the left Coptic link and then up and around the cover at station 4. Link to the cover as you did in step 26. Continue sewing over the final tape. Finish with a true kettle stitch link to the previous signature. Leave the thread long (H). It will be used to attach the covers.

32. Center each tape by gently rocking beneath the threads so an equal amount of the tape hangs off the front and back of the text block. Gently tuck the edges of the tapes beneath the cover boards.

33. Use the thread's tails to attach the covers (see Attaching the Covers, page 25). Tie off the loose threads in the inside of the nearest signature (see Tying Off the Binding, page 27).

ATTACH A BUTTON

34. Place the button on the front cover and arrange it so it so its edge is ¼ inch (6 mm) away from the fore edge of the cover. Use an awl to lightly mark the holes of the button onto the cover (I).

35. Set the button aside. Punch through the marked holes on the cover with the awl. Use a needle and 8 inches (20.3 cm) of button thread to sew the button in place. Knot on the inside of the board and trim the tails to ¼ inch (6 mm).

36. On the back cover, use an awl to punch a hole ¼ inch (6 mm) from the fore edge of the cover in alignment with the button on the front cover. Cut a piece of button thread 16 inches (40.6 cm) long. Guide one end of the thread through the hole. Pull both ends of the thread so they are even. Fasten the thread with a square knot near the edge of the cover (J).

37. Fasten the cover by wrapping the loose ends of the thread around the button on the front cover.

STRIP STRIPED

The covers of this mini journal are constructed from
the text block of a steamy Japanese romance novel.
Of course, it was stripped down to its bare essentials.

finished dimensions

3 x 4 x ½ inches (7.6 x 10.2 x 1.3 cm)

stitches used

True kettle stitch (page 24); running stitch (page 20); gathering stitch (page 24); over-hand stitch (page 28)

what you need

Basic Bookmaking Toolkit (page 13)

Bookbinding thread, 36 inches (91 cm)

Upcycled text block, at least 5 x 7 inches (12.7 x 17.8 cm)

Corner rounder

2 sheets of cardboard

10 sheets of text-weight paper, 8½ x 11 inches (21.6 x 27.9 cm)

Cardstock for the hole-punch guide

Four 25-inch (63.5 cm) lengths of binder's thread for binding and embellishing the cover

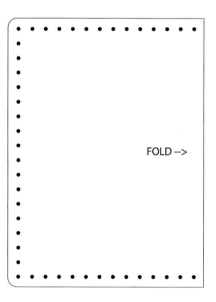

template 1
3 x 4 inches (7.6 x 10.2 cm)

Enlarge template by 30%

PREPARE THE COVER

1. Strip 20 pages from the upcycled text block and divide the pages into two stacks of 10. Each of these stacks will be bound together to make a cover.

2. Using a paper cutter, cut each stack to 6 x 4 inches (15.2 x 10.2 cm).

3. Fold each stack to 3 x 4 inches (7.6 x 10.2 cm) using a bone folder to smooth the folded edge. The fore edge of the folded covers may form a V shape and extend beyond the edges of the outer pages. If this occurs, trim the fore edges to bring the width back to 3 inches (7.6 cm).

4. Using the corner rounder, round the two outer corners of each folded cover.

5. Create a cardstock punch guide (page 17) for the cover using Template 1. Align the punch guide to the outside of the front cover so the fold on the guide is aligned to the fold of the cover and place both on top of a double layer of cardboard to protect the table surface. Use the awl to punch holes through the cover. Repeat for the back cover. Be sure to punch with the outside of the covers facing up so that the outside surface will remain smooth.

MAKE THE SIGNATURES

6. Cut all ten sheets of text-weight paper in half so you have 20 sheets measuring 8½ x 5½ inches (21.6 x 14 cm). Divide the paper into five stacks of four sheets. Jog each pile and fold it in half to make a 4¼ x 5½ inch (10.8 x 14 cm) signature, creasing with the bone folder. There will be five signatures total.

7. Using the paper cutter, trim the fore edge of each signature so the width remains 3 inches (7.6 cm) and trim the height to 4 inches (10 cm).

8. Using the corner rounder, round the two outer corners of each signature.

PUNCH HOLES IN THE COVERS AND SIGNATURES

9. To create a cardstock hole-punch guide, use Template 2. Fold it in half lengthwise so it measures 1 x 4 inches. Use the awl to punch the marked holes in the guide.

10. Nest the cardstock punch guide within a cover, making certain the edges are aligned. Hold the signature and the guide securely in alignment. Push the awl through all six sewing stations. Repeat for the other cover and each signature.

ASSEMBLE THE BOOK

11. Starting with the top cover, sew the text block together using the running stitch binding method, with true kettle stitches to link the top and bottom sewing stations of each signature together. Be sure to leave at least 2 inches (5.1 cm) of loose thread at sewing station 1.

12. On the final signature, exit from sewing station 2.

13. Make a gathering stitch (page 24).

14. Continue into sewing station 4 and repeat the gathered stitch in the same way as above. Complete the binding with a true kettle stitch at the end station (A).

15. To tie off, enter through the last sewing station and tie off inside (see Tying Off the Binding, page 27). Repeat for the remaining loose thread.

STITCH THE COVER

16. Attach one end of each of the four lengths of thread on the inside of the cover using a square knot (page 28), one at each of sewing stations 1 and 6.

17. Choose one of the threads to begin. Thread the needle and begin sewing the cover together using the overhand stitch method. Start by inserting the needle down through the first outside hole nearest the spine. Pull thread and wrap it around to enter through the second outer hole.

18. Continue sewing in this manner until you reach the center hole on the fore edge of the cover.

19. Remove the needle and leave the loose end of the thread. Put the needle on the loose end of thread at the other side of the cover and repeat the overhand stitch instructions. Once you have completed this, you'll have two loose threads hanging from the center holes.

20. Make a square knot on the inside of the cover. Trim each thread to 5 inches (12.7 cm).

21. Repeat the above instruction for the remaining cover. Tie the remaining threads together to fasten the book.

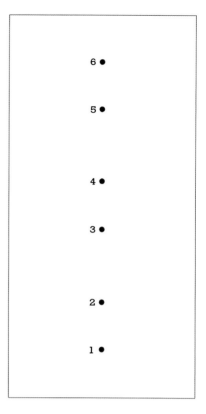

template 2
2 x 4 inches (5.1 x 10.2 cm)

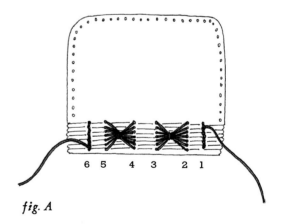

fig. A

WARMLY YOURS

A book of your own filled with a story of your own, wrapped in your comfy old sweater. Doesn't that sound cozy?

finished dimensions

7 x 4⅛ x 1¼ inches (17.8 x 10.5 x 3.2 cm)

stitches used

Long stitch (page 21), gathering stitch (page 24)

what you need

Basic Bookmaking Toolkit (page 13)

Bookbinding thread, 40 inches (102 cm)

15 sheets of 300g handmade paper, 4 x 12¼ inches (10.2 x 31.1 cm)

2 decorative end sheets, 4 x 7 inches (10.2 x 17.8 cm)

Binder's board, ¾ x 4 inches (1.9 x 10.2 cm), 3/16 inch (5 mm) thick

1 decorative sheet, 1½ x 5 inches (3.8 x 12.7 cm)

1 sheet of cardstock

3/32-inch (2.3 mm) hole punch

Felted wool from an old sweater, 4⅛ x 16½ inches (10.5 x 41.9 cm)

Marker or cloth pen with disappearing ink (optional)

16 inches (40.6 cm) button thread

Sewing needle

Drawing paper (optional)

Sewing machine and thread or sewing needle with embroidery floss (optional)

1 button (optional)

4 3-inch pieces of button thread

Tip: Match the color of the decorative sheet and the end sheets for a cohesive look. Also be sure the sweater is completely felted so the raw edges of the cover do not unravel.

MAKE THE TEXT BLOCK

1. Make five signatures of three sheets each, measuring 4 x 6⅛ inches (10.2 x 15.5 cm). Because the paper is heavy weight, be sure to fold each sheet individually first and then rest into signatures. Use the bone folder to crease the fold lines.

2. Add the decorative end sheets to the front side of the first signature and the back side of the last signature. To do this, align the bottom 4-inch (10.2 cm) edge of the top end sheet to the fore edge of the first signature. Wrap the top ¾ inch (1.9 cm) of the end sheet around the fold of the signature (see figure A, page 135). Repeat these steps to add the bottom end sheet.

PUNCH THE SIGNATURES

3. Create a punch guide with cardstock from the Template 1. Nest the template in the centerfold of each signature, place the signature in the gutter of an opened phonebook, and punch the holes with an awl. Stack the signatures in order and place them to the side.

PREPARE THE SPINE PIECE

4. Place a 6 x 6-inch (15.2 x 15.2 cm) protective sheet of wax or craft paper on your work surface. Place the binder's board on the paper.

5. Use a brush to apply a thin layer of glue to one side of the binder's board.

6. Center the board, glue side down, onto the back of the 1½ x 5-inch (3.8 x 12.7 cm) decorative sheet. Press the board to the sheet and then turn it over and use a bone folder to smooth any air bubbles.

7. Turn the board over so the bare side is faceup. Use a ruler to measure ⅛ inch (3 mm) from the tip of each of the four corners of the board and mark this distance with a pencil. Use a ruler to draw diagonal lines that will be cut to remove the corners of the decorative paper (A).

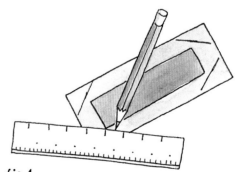

fig.A

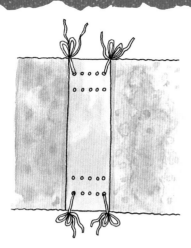

fig. B

fig. C

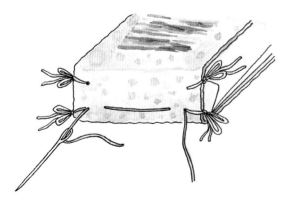

fig. D

8. Use scissors to trim the corners along the diagonal marks.

9. Use a small brush to apply glue to one of the longer edges of the decorative sheet. Fold the edge over to cover the edge of the back of the board and smooth it with a bone folder. Repeat for the opposite edge and then the remaining shorter edges.

10. Create a template with cardstock from Template 2 and place it on the covered side of the spine piece. Use a pencil to mark the holes.

11. Use the hole punch to puncture the marks.

PREPARE THE COVER

12. Place the felted wool facedown on your work surface. Arrange the text block (faceup) and spine board (faceup so the raw edge of the board is next to the wool) on the wool piece, a little left of center. The left end of the wool should line up with the fore edge of the text block when you fold it over, and of course the spine board should be in place between wool and the spine edge of the text block.

13. Carefully open the top wool cover again to reveal the spine board. Remove the text block and set it aside.

14. Using a needle and the 3-inch lengths of button thread, temporarily fasten the spine board to the wool in its bound position by tying each of the four corner holes to their position on the wool. You will have a total of four ties that will later be removed (B).

DECORATE THE COVER (OPTIONAL)

15. Measure the cover area that you wish to decorate. Mark the dimensions on a piece of drawing paper and sketch your design onto the paper.

16. When you are satisfied with the design, use a sewing machine or hand-stitch with embroidery floss and a needle to transfer the design onto the wool cover.

TIP: You may consider practicing on a spare piece of wool before sewing the final version. Since wool can be quite thick, use bold lines, and if sewing by hand, use thick embroidery floss or wool thread. My version of the book was decorated using the embroidery setting on a sewing machine, which makes very narrow zigzags to form bold lines.

ASSEMBLE THE BOOK

17. To bind the book, spread the cover open with the inside facing up and the front cover toward you. Pull the bottom signature from the text block and align it with the bottom row of sewing stations in the spine piece (C).

18. Using a needle single-threaded with 40 inches of binder's thread, gently locate sewing station 1 on the spine board through the outside of the wool cover. Once you locate it, enter into it and draw the needle through it and into the corresponding sewing station on the first signature.

19. Pull the thread taut, leaving a 4-inch (10.2 cm) tail of thread on the outside of the cover.

20. Enter sewing station 2 from inside the signature and pull the thread through the corresponding spine board sewing station 2 to the outside of the cover.

21. With the tip of the needle, locate sewing station 3 and push the needle through it. Pull the thread into the center of the signature.

22. Enter sewing station 4 and pull the thread to the outside of the cover (D).

23. Continue to the next signature and follow the long stitch sewing pattern to complete the binding.

OPTIONAL: When sewing the fifth signature, you may consider making a gathering stitch between sewing stations 2 and 3 to connect the previous threads for ornamentation.

TIE OFF THE BINDING

24. When the sewing pattern is complete, draw the thread into the nearest hole and pull the thread taut. Tie off (see page 27) on the inside and trim the tail to ¼ inch (6 mm).

25. Thread the needle on the remaining tail on the outside of the spine and repeat step 24 to complete the binding.

26. Remove the temporary strings that you used earlier to attach the spine piece to the cover.

FASTEN THE COVER

27. There are a couple of options for fastening the wrap around cover. The felt may naturally cling to its own fibers, so no additional closure may be necessary. If this is not the case for your wool book, consider cutting a small slit in the wraparound cover to use as a buttonhole. Attach a vintage button to the underlying cover directly beneath the buttonhole. Your book will then fasten securely!

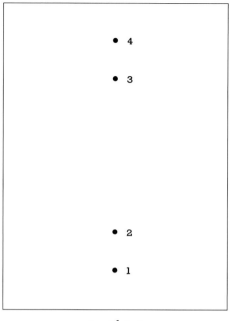

template 1
3 x 4 inches (7.6 x 10.2 cm)

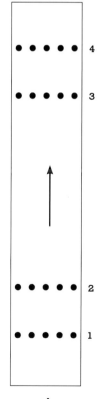

template 2
¾ x 4 inches

NATURE
BOOKS

BOOK OF THE SEA

May the sea be with you in this totemic binding.

CHOOSE THE COVER

1. Choose a type of shell that is strong enough to be handled without cracking or breaking. If you can crack or break the shell by bending it with your hands, it is not adequate for this project. Clam, scallop, and cockle shells are excellent choices for this project. For sourcing shells, see page 10.

DRILL THE COVER

2. Mark holes for drilling on either side of the hinge; they should be approximately 2¼ inches (5.7 cm) apart on a larger shell and 1½ inches (3.8 cm) apart on a smaller shell. The hole on the shorter edge of the umbo should be set within ½ inch (1.3 cm) of the umbo, and the hole on the long edge should be placed on the outer edge of the hinge. Mark both holes ³⁄₁₆ inch (5 mm) from edge (A). To mark identical marks on the other shell half, fit the shells together and mark matching holes.

3. Fill the water tub or sink with enough room-temperature water to fully submerge the height of the shell.

4. Put on your safety glasses and dust mask. Using an electric drill fitted with a diamond cylinder tip, fully submerge one half shell beneath the water and, with the drill set on high speed, carefully drill through each hole, working from the outside in. Make sure the shell and drill tip remain submerged so the shell dust does not become airborne—you don't want to inhale it. Drill the remaining half shell. Dry both half shells with a towel.

MAKE THE SIGNATURES

5. Divide the paper into nine stacks of four sheets each. Fold each stack into a signature that measures 4 x 2¾ inches (10.2 x 7 cm).

6. To make a template for shaping the signatures, place one signature on your work surface and align the holes of one half shell to the folded edge of the signature. With an awl, trace the contour of the shell with enough pressure to leave a mark as a cutting guide (B).

finished dimensions

Depends on the size of shell.
Maximum size: 2¾ x 4 inches (7 x 10.2 cm);
Minimum size: 1½ x 3 inches (3.8 x 7.6 cm)

stitches used

True kettle stitch (page 24), Coptic stitch (page 22)

what you need

Basic Bookmaking Toolkit (page 13)

Bookbinding thread, 55 inches (140 cm)

Clam shell, 4 x 2¾ inches (10.2 x 7 cm) or smaller

Water tub or sink

Safety glasses

Dust mask

Electric drill with 2.55 mm diamond cylinder drill bit

Towel

36 sheets of text-weight paper, 4 x 5½ inches (10.2 x 14 cm)

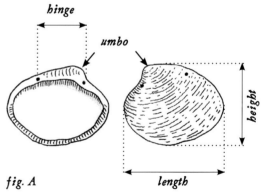

fig. A

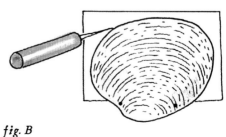

fig. B

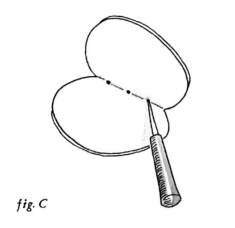

fig. C

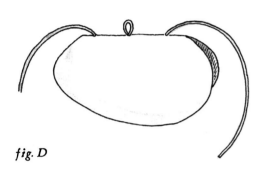

fig. D

fig. E

fig. F

7. Using scissors, cut along the guide you created on the signature; this will be your tracing guide for the remaining signatures. Align the fold of this guide signature to the fold of the remaining signatures (one at a time) and gently trace the contour with an awl.

8. Using scissors, cut each signature along the guideline as smoothly and accurately as possible.

PUNCH THE HOLES

9. To mark the sewing stations, align the inner fold of one signature to one half shell and, with a pencil, lightly mark the placement of the two holes on the inner fold of the signature. For the center hole, find the center point between the other marks. Pierce each of the three marks with an awl. The interior folded sheet of this punched signature will serve as a punch guide for the remaining signatures.

10. Nest the punch guide within each signature and carefully punch the holes (C). When you're finished, return the punch guide to the interior of the signature from which it came.

ASSEMBLE THE BOOK

11. Line up all nine signatures into a text block, making certain they all face the same direction. Beginning with the top signature and the leftmost sewing station, sew the text block together using the Coptic stitch binding method (D, E), and use true kettle stitches to link the top and bottom sewing stations of each signature together. Be sure to leave at least 12 inches (30.5 cm) of loose thread at the first and final sewing stations for attaching the covers (F).

12. Attach the covers (page 25). Finish by tying off the threads in the inside of the nearest signature (page 27).

LEAFLET

Nature is most profound, especially when it drops sagely messages
to be discovered by those who least expect them. Scatter these
ephemeral leaflets around your home, neighborhood, or place
of work—wherever you want to shed a little light.

finished dimensions

Depends on leaf size

stitch used

Pamphlet stitch (page 20)

what you need

Basic Bookmaking Toolkit (page 13)

4 sheets of text-weight paper, dimensions equal to the height and width of the leaf

1 oval-shaped leaf, minimum 2 x 3 inches (see Tip after step 5)

Writing utensil or typewriter (see suggestions in step 6)

Gold or natural thread, four times the length of the leaf's midrib

Tip: Choose a leaf that is strong yet pliable—blackberry, raspberry and sunflower leaves are good choices. After the leaf is harvested, it should be used immediately so it is pliable enough to fold along the midrib without cracking.

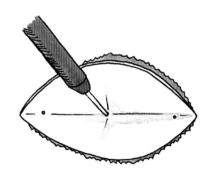

fig.A

PREPARE THE COVER

1. Set the stack of paper beside the leaf and orient it so the dimensions mirror those of the leaf. Use a bone folder to fold the stacked paper into a signature with the fold line running the same direction as the midrib of the leaf.

MAKE THE TEXT BLOCK

2. Gently fold the leaf in half along its midrib.

3. Nest the signature within the leaf and place it on your work surface with one of the covers facing up.

4. Use an awl or pencil to trace the outline of the leaf into the signature. If the leaf has a jagged edge, you may choose to follow the edges or simplify with a smooth line. Remove the signature from the cover.

5. Use scissors to cut along the outline on the top of the signature.

TIP: Most leaves will shrink in size as they dry. If you prefer your signature to fit within the leaf covers after it has dried, use scissors to cut off another ¼ inch from the curved edge of the signature.

ADD CONTENT

6. Write or type your content onto the pages of the signature. Some ideas: use a typewriter, colored pencils, ink and brush, or a gold pen to write your message; see the quote inspirations throughout. Be sure to keep the pages in order.

PUNCH THE HOLES

7. To determine the sewing stations, open the signature to the centerfold. Measure ½ inch (1.3 cm) from the top and bottom edges on the fold line and mark with a pencil. Find the center of the fold line and mark with a pencil.

8. Nest the signature into the cover. Fold the signature open and use an awl to gently punch through the marked stations. You may need to direct the awl to one side of the leaf midrib if it is difficult to punch through it (A).

ASSEMBLE THE BOOK

9. Sew the binding with a basic pamphlet stitch.

10. Once you're done binding, position the thread ends so they are on opposite sides of the long wraparound stitch that runs the length of the leaf's midrib.

11. Pull the thread ends taut and tie them off near the middle hole with a square knot (page 28). If the ends of the threads are uneven, trim them even. Leave the ends long and loose for securing the pamphlet closed or for hanging (B).

12. Press the closed leaflet in a botanical press or between the pages of a heavy book until dry: 2–5 days depending on the humidity of your location and the water content in the leaf.

13. Use or give the leaflet immediately, as the dried leaf will become more brittle as time passes and eventually succumb to decomposition.

fig.B

FUGITIVE INK

*Don't want to be held accountable? This homemade sepia ink
will fade or disappear over time. It's made to use with a dipping
pen for writing or with a paintbrush for lightly washing over
your paper and giving it an aged, distressed look.*

you will need

5 tea bags or 5 teaspoons of loose black tea in
a tea ball or strainer

1 large teacup

½ cup (118 ml) of boiling water

1 teaspoon powdered gum arabic

Strainer

Glass ink bottle

1. Place the tea in a cup and pour boiling water over the tea. Allow
   the tea to steep for 25 minutes.

2. Squeeze the tea bags or mash the tea in the strainer. This will
   release the remaining tannins from the tea leaves.

3. Stir in the gum arabic.

4. Strain the ink into the ink bottle and allow it to cool to room
   temperature.

5. Cap and store in cool, dark location. Use immediately or within
   two weeks.

THE DRIFTER

Like a beach, your home can be a welcome place for any
weary traveler of the land or sea. Make a space for thanks
in between a couple of driftwood or reclaimed lumber planks.

finished dimensions

Depends upon the size of reclaimed wood.

stitches used

Running stitch (page 20), Coptic stitch (page 22), true kettle stitch (page 24)

what you need

Basic Bookmaking Toolkit (page 13)

Lumber driftwood or reclaimed milled board with visible wood grain, approximately 10 x 6 x ½ inches (25.4 x 15.2 x 1.3 cm)

Dust mask

Wood clamps (optional)

Handsaw

Cloth rag

Medium-fine sandpaper

Wood-burning tool

Sheet of cardstock; 8½ x 11 inches (21.6 x 27.9 cm)

Scratch paper

45 sheets of text-weight paper, 8½ x 11 inches (21.6 x 27.9 cm)

Cardstock for the template

Piece of scrap wood, minimum size 6 x 6 x ½ inches (15.2 x 15.2 x 1.3 cm)

Handheld wood drill with ¹⁄₁₆-inch (1.6 mm) wood bit

Note: I advise being in a well-ventilated area and using a dust mask for at least the sawing portion of this project in order to keep from breathing in sawdust.

MAKE THE COVERS

1. Place the board faceup on your work surface.

2. Use a ruler to measure the width of the board. Mark the center of it at the top and bottom edges with a pencil. Use the metal ruler to draw a vertical line between the points. The line will mark the center of the board.

3. Protect your lungs with a dust mask and move to a ventilated area appropriate for sawing your board, such as a garage or outdoor area.

4. Place the board horizontally on a sturdy surface with two-thirds of the board hanging off the edge. Hold the edge of the board firmly to the surface with one hand and, if possible, one knee. (If tools are available, you may also clamp the boards firmly to the surface with board clamps.)

5. With your other hand, use the saw to cut along the midline. Completely saw through the board in a straight line until it's divided into two equal halves. Brush the dust from the boards with the cloth rag.

6. Lightly sand the surface and edges of the boards to remove any rough surfaces.

7. Still working in a ventilated area, use the rag to brush the dust from the boards and place them on a working space.

8. Turn on your wood-burning tool and allow it to heat up.

9. Use a pencil to draw the pattern you wish to burn onto the covers. You may consider simply tracing the pattern of the wood grain or you may create a more elaborate design.

10. Use the wood burner to burn the drawn pattern into your boards by tracing over the pencil lines.

11. Turn off the wood burner and set it aside safely for cooling. Remove your mask and return to your normal work area.

MAKE THE SIGNATURES

12. To determine the dimensions of the pages for the journals, choose one of the cover boards and measure the width and height. Write this measurement on a piece of scratch paper. Subtract ¼ inch (6 mm) from the height. This is the height of the signature. Multiply the width of the cover board by two and subtract ¼ inch (6 mm) from the total. This is the width of the signature.

13. With your paper cutter, cut 45 sheets of text-weight paper to the determined measurements. Separate the sheets into nine piles of five.

14. Use the bone folder to fold each stack into a signature.

CREATE A PUNCH GUIDE

15. Determine the dimension of the guide; it will be the same height as your signature and 3 inches (7.6 cm) wide. Cut the template from the sheet of cardstock to the determined size. Make a vertical fold in the template. Smooth the crease with your bone folder.

16. Open the template and place it on your work surface.

17. Measure ¾ inch (1.9 cm) from the top and bottom of the guide, and use a pencil to mark these points along the fold line. Then measure ½ inch (1.3 cm) to the inside of both of the first marks and mark there. Mark more points ¾ inch (1.9 cm) in from the previous marks. The final mark will be in the center of the spine. You should have a total of seven marks. Draw an arrow on the inside of the guide to signify the upright position.

PUNCH HOLES IN THE SIGNATURES

18. Nest the punch guide, with the arrow pointing upright, inside each of the signatures and punch the holes with your awl. Stack the signatures and set them aside.

DRILL HOLES IN THE COVER BOARDS

19. Choose one signature and sandwich it between the cover boards so it aligns as it would if bound.

20. Slide one of the cover boards ¼ inch (6 mm) away from the spine of the signature so the sewing stations are visible. Make certain the top and bottom edges of the signature are centered within the edges of the board.

21. Use a pencil to mark on the cover board where to drill holes that will align to the top, middle, and bottom sewing stations of the signature. The marks should be ¼ inch (6 mm) in from the spine edge. Flip the entire stack over and repeat for the remaining board. Each board will have three marks.

22. Return to your ventilated work area and put on a dust mask.

23. Place one of the boards on a piece of scrap wood. Use a handheld drill to make holes through the three marks on the cover board. Be sure to hold the drill in an upright 90° position while drilling so the holes are straight. Repeat the above steps for the remaining cover board.

24. Dust off the boards and remove your dust mask. Return to your normal work area.

ASSEMBLE THE BOOK

25. Align the signatures within the covers and place them on your work surface.

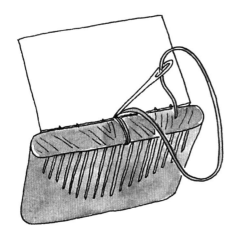

fig. A

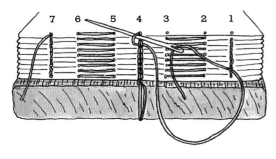

fig. B

26. Determine the length of thread by measuring the height of the signature. Multiply the height of the spine by nine and add 20 inches (50.8 cm). This is the amount of thread needed to sew the book.

27. Pull the bottom signature and cover board from the stack. Enter your threaded needle into the outside of the rightmost sewing station on the signature and pull it into the inside of the signature. Pull the needle until there is a 10-inch (25.4 cm) tail of thread remaining on the outside of the signature.

28. Enter the thread into the second sewing station and pull it to the outside of the signature. Continue sewing in running stitch until your needle is on the outside of the center sewing station.

29. Pull the thread around the outside of the cover and into its center hole. Loop it around the center station on the cover twice. Return the needle to the center sewing station of the signature and guide it to the interior of the signature (A).

30. Continue in running stitch until you reach the leftmost sewing station. Pull the next signature from the stack and direct-link it to the previous one by guiding the needle into its nearest sewing station.

31. Continue sewing the remaining signatures with running stitches between stations 2 and 3 and stations 5 and 6. Station 4 (the center station) will link to the previous signature with a Coptic stitch. The end stations will link to previous signatures with true kettle stitches.

32. Once you reach the center station in the final signature, finish by linking it to the previous signature with a Coptic stitch. Instead of guiding the needle back into the center hole, guide it beneath the thread linking the center stations of signatures 8 and 9 (B). Pull the thread until taut.

ATTACH THE COVERS AND TIE OFF THE BINDING

33. Place the remaining cover board on top of the final signature.

34. Guide the needle around the outside of the cover and into the center hole of the board. Loop it around the center station on the board twice. Return the needle to the center sewing station of the final signature and complete the running-stitch sewing pattern to the last station and link to the previous signature with a true kettle stitch.

35. Use the loose tail threads to attach the covers (page 25). Tie off the loose threads (page 27) in the inside of the nearest signature and trim the tails to ¼ inch (6 mm).

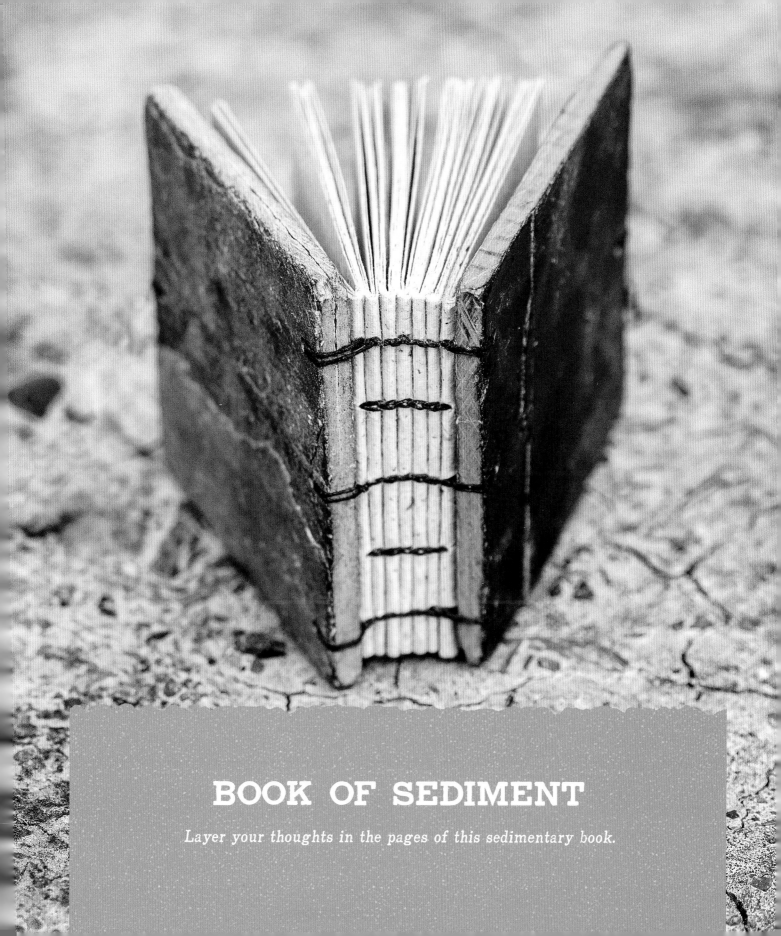

BOOK OF SEDIMENT

Layer your thoughts in the pages of this sedimentary book.

finished dimensions

3¾ x 3¾ x 1½ inches (9.5 x 9.5 x 3.8 cm)

stitches used

Coptic stitch (page 22), true kettle stitch (page 24)

what you need

Basic Bookmaking Toolkit (page 13)

Bookbinding thread, 54 inches (137 cm)

2 slate tiles, approximately 3¾ x 3¾ inches (9.5 x 9.5 cm) each

Water tub or sink

Safety glasses

Dust mask

Electric drill with 2.55 mm diamond cylinder drill bit

Towel

21 sheets of handmade paper, 7 x 3½ inches (17.8 x 8.9 cm)

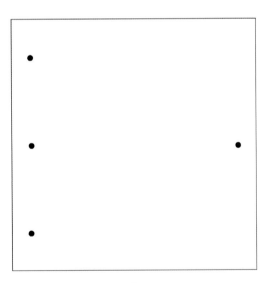

template 1
3¾ x 3¾ inches (9.5 x 9.5 cm)

Enlarge template by 30%

DRILL THE COVERS

1. With a pencil and using Template 1, mark four holes on each slate tile. Each hole should be set ¼ inch (6 mm) from the edge of the tile.

2. Fill the water tub with enough water (cold or warm) to fully submerge the tile. Put on the safety glasses and dust mask.

3. Fully submerge one tile beneath water and carefully drill through each hole with the electric drill on high speed. Make sure the tile and drill tip remain submerged while drilling so the stone dust does not become airborne and get inhaled into your lungs. Drill the remaining tile. Dry both tiles with a towel.

MAKE THE SIGNATURES

4. Individually fold all sheets in half to measure 3½ x 3½ inches (8.9 x 8.9 cm). Use a bone folder to crease the folds. Nest three folded sheets together to make one six-page signature. Continue to nest all the sheets until you have a total of seven signatures.

PUNCH THE HOLES

5. Create a punch guide (page 17) using Template 2. Nest the guide within the center of each signature within the gutter of an open phonebook, and punch the holes with an awl.

ASSEMBLE THE BOOK

6. Stack the punched signatures in the order you want them to be in the book.

7. Begin sewing signature 1: Draw the threaded needle into sewing station 1 and out through sewing station 2, leaving 8 inches (20.3 cm) of thread hanging loose outside station 1.

8. Reenter through the second station and form a loop that will be used to link the following signature.

9. Draw the needle and thread out through the center sewing station (3) and wrap it twice around the cover spine through the center hole in the tile.

10. Reenter sewing station 3 (A).

11. Draw the needle and thread out through the sewing station 4 and, as you did at the second station, reenter through the same sewing station to form a loop that will be used to link the following signature.

12. Draw the needle out through sewing station 5.

13. Sew signature 2: Direct link into sewing station 5 and out through station 4.

14. At sewing station 4, link through the open loop and pull the threads taut (B).

15. Reenter through sewing station 4 and exit through the center one.

16. Link the center sewing stations with a basic Coptic stitch and reenter the center sewing station (C).

17. In the next sewing station (2), again draw the thread through the loop to link the signatures. Pull the slack thread taut.

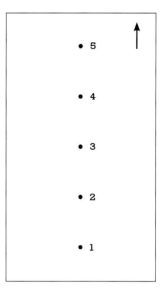

template 2
2 x 3¾ inches (5.1 x 9.5 cm)

Enlarge template by 20%

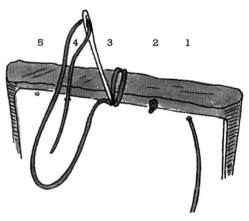

fig. A

5 4 3 2 1

fig. B

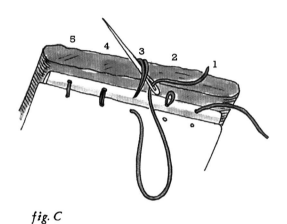

5 4 3 2 1

fig. C

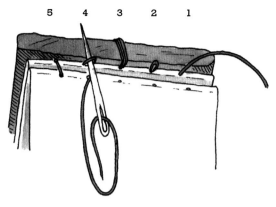

5
4
3
2
1

fig. D

18. Reenter through the same sewing station (2) and out through station 1. Link the first and second signatures with a square knot (page 28) (D).

19. Signatures 3 through 7: Continue with the basic Coptic stitch method.

20. After linking the seventh signature's center Coptic stitch to the sixth signature, guide the thread beneath the thread linking the center stations of signatures 6 and 7. Draw the needle through the outer hole of the center cover hole and wrap around the cover edge twice.

21. Reenter the needle through the center hole of the signature (station 3) and continue with the basic Coptic stitch method. Be sure to leave 8 inches (20.3 cm) of loose thread at the end of the last signature for tying off.

22. Secure the covers (see Attaching the Covers, page 25) and tie off the loose threads (see Tying Off the Binding, page 27).

ATTACH THE TIES

23. Fold one 18-inch (45.7 cm) length of binder's thread in half for each cover. Draw the loose ends of the thread through the center hole on the fore edge of the cover and pull it through the loop on the other end of the thread forming a lark's head knot (page 28). Pull it taut. Secure the knot with a square knot (page 28). Trim the thread to 5 inches (12.7 cm). Repeat for the other cover.

QUARTER YEAR
MOON JOURNAL

The moon has a rhythm all her own. Get to know her ups and downs with this lunar cycle–inspired journal, good for four whole moons.

finished dimensions

2½ x 5 x 1¼ inches (6.4 x 12.7 x 3.2 cm)

stitches used

Running stitch (page 20), Coptic stitch
(page 22), gathering stitch (page 24),
true kettle stitch (page 24)

what you need

Basic Bookmaking Toolkit (page 13)

Bookbinding thread, 116 inches (295 cm)

Moon template (page 89)

1 sheet of white writing paper; 8½ x 11 inches
(21.6 x 27.9 cm)

2 black museum boards, 3 x 5 x ¹⁄₁₆ inch (7.6
cm x 12.7 cm x 1.6 mm)

Black binder's thread, 116 inches (294.6 cm)

16 sheets of black writing paper, 5½ x 5½
inches (14 x 14 cm)

16 sheets of white writing paper, 5½ x 5½
inches (14 x 14 cm)

32 sheets of silver or gray writing paper,
5½ x 5½ inches (14 x 14 cm)

1 sheet of cardstock, 3 x 5½ inches
(7.6 x 14 cm)

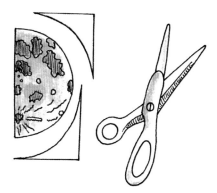

fig. A

PREPARE THE COVER

1. Photocopy the vintage image from Template 1 at 100 percent onto the 8 ½ x 11-inch (21.6 x 27.9 cm) white writing paper.

2. Use scissors to cut out the moon graphic.

3. Fold the moon in half to locate the center line. Use a paper cutter to cut the moon in half along the folded line.

4. Place a piece of wax paper on your work surface. Position one half moon back side up on the wax paper.

5. Apply a thin coat of glue to the back of the half moon. Adhere it to one of the black boards with the long edges of the moon and board aligned. Use a bone folder to smooth any air bubbles. Repeat for the remaining half moon and black board.

6. Use scissors to cut the moon from the boards (A). Set the covers aside.

MAKE THE TEXT BLOCK

7. Divide the black writing paper into four stacks of four sheets. Use your bone folder to fold each stack into a signature measuring 2¾ x 5½ inches (7 x 14 cm). Repeat for the white and silver/gray sheets. You should have four white signatures, four black signatures, and eight silver/gray signatures.

NOTE: White is representative of the full moon; black, the new moon; and silver/gray, the waning and waxing cycles of the moon phases.

8. Place one of the signatures on your work surface. Position one of the cover boards on the signature with the straight edge of the cover aligned to the spine of the signature.

9. Use an awl to trace the contour of the round cover board edge onto the signature below. Apply just enough pressure with the awl to leave a mark on the paper.

10. Use scissors to cut along the traced contour of the signature.

11. Use the cut signature as a template to trace the contour on the remaining signatures.

12. Use a scissors to cut along the traced contour of the remaining signatures.

13. Arrange the signatures in the following order: black, gray/silver, white, gray/silver; repeat this pattern with the remaining signatures.

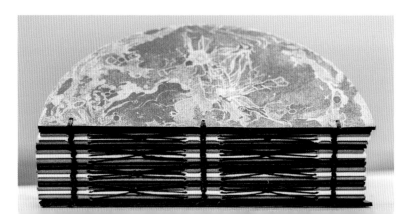

template 1
5 x 5 inches (12.7 x 12.7 cm)

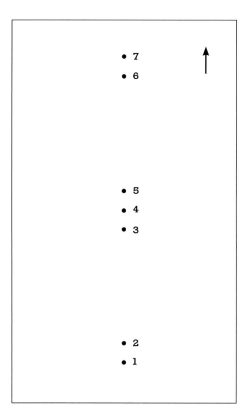

template 2
3 x 5 inches (7.6 x 12.7 cm)

Enlarge template by 20%

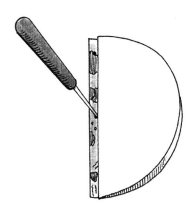

fig. B

PUNCH HOLES IN THE SIGNATURES

14. Use the sheet of cardstock to create a punch template (see page 17) from Template 2.

15. Nest the punch template inside each signature, nest the signature in the gutter of an open phonebook, and use an awl to punch all sewing stations. After each signature is punched, arrange them in order again.

PUNCH HOLES IN THE COVERS

16. Choose a signature and lay it on the top cover board with the spine edges and top and bottom edges aligned. Shift the signature spine ¼ inch (6 mm) inside the edge of the cover board.

17. Use an awl to mark the position of the top, bottom, and center holes of the signature onto the board (B). Set the signature aside.

18. Use the awl to punch through the marks on the cover board.

19. Lay both cover boards on the work surface. Align the spine edges of the covers so the boards form a circle.

20. Use an awl to mark matching holes on the unpunched cover ¼ inch (6 mm) from the spine edge (C).

21. Pick up the board and punch completely through the holes.

ASSEMBLE THE BOOK

22. Prepare the text block for binding. Make certain all signatures are in order and nest the text block inside the cover boards. Pull the top cover and first signature from the stack.

23. To bind signature 1, draw the threaded needle into sewing station 1 and pull the thread inside the signature, leaving a 16-inch (40.6 cm) tail on the outside for attaching the covers.

24. Continue sewing with a running stitch until you reach the outside of the center hole. Loop twice around the outside of the center hole in the cover. Reenter the center stewing station in the signature.

25. Again, continue with a running stitch until you reach the outside of sewing station 7.

26. Direct link into station 7 of the next signature and continue sewing with the running stitch (page 20). Link to the loose thread at sewing station 1 with a square knot (page 28) (D).

27. To bind signatures 3, 5, 6, 7, 9, 10, 11, and 13, 14, 15, pull the next signature from the stack and position it next to the sewn signature. Draw the needle into the closest sewing station and continue sewing the signature with a running stitch. At the center station (4), link to the previous signature with a Coptic stitch and reenter into the center hole. Then continue with a running stitch. Link the top and bottom of the signatures with a true kettle stitch.

28. To bind signatures 4, 8, and 12, pull the next signature from the stack and position it next to the previously sewn signature. Draw the needle into the closest sewing station and continue sewing the signature with a running stitch. Make a gathering stitch between stations 2 and 3 and stations 5 and 6 by gathering the thread of the three previous signatures. Continue to link the center station with a Coptic stitch and link the signature with a true kettle stitch (E).

29. In signature 16, make a gathering stitch between stations 2 and 3.

30. Draw the thread to the outside of the center hole and make a Coptic link to the previous signature.

31. Draw the needle beneath the thread of the center hole between signatures 15 and 16. Pull the thread taut and guide the needle around the outside of the cover's spine edge. Wrap around the center hole of the cover twice. Enter into the center hole of signature 16.

32. Make a gathering stitch between stations 5 and 6 and complete the binding by linking to the previous signature with a true kettle stitch at station 7. Leave the needle threaded.

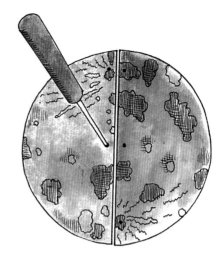

fig. C

ATTACH THE COVERS

33. Because this binding has an even number of signatures (page 26), the method for attaching the covers has a slight variation.

34. Attach the cover that is nearest the thread (see Attaching a Cover, page 25) and hike the needle down the spine to the back cover (see hiking, page 25). Do not attach this cover; instead, enter into the nearest signature and tie off in the inside of the signature (see Tying Off the Binding, page 27). Trim the thread to ¼ inch (6 mm).

35. Thread the needle to the remaining tail.

36. Attach the nearest cover and enter into the nearest hole. Pull the thread into the center of the signature. Draw the thread to the other end of signature and through the last station to the outside of the signature. Pull the thread taut.

37. Attach the nearest cover and hike the needle down the spine to the other cover. Attach the cover and enter into the nearest hole. Tie off in the inside of the signature. Trim the thread to ¼ inch (6 mm).

TIP: If you cannot find a source for black-colored boards, consider using regular book board and apply two or three washes of black India Ink for boards "as dark as night."

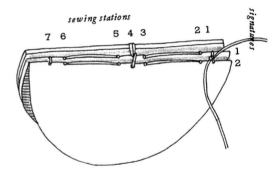

fig. D

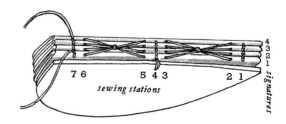

fig. E

LAST YEAR'S VIOLET

Say it with flowers. Here is a delicate pamphlet for
sharing your tender thoughts, poetry, or prose.

MAKE THE SIGNATURE

1. Use a bone folder to fold the stack of text-weight paper into a signature that measures approximately 2⅞ x 4 inches (7.3 x 10.2 cm).

MAKE THE COVER

2. Turn on the iron and set it to medium heat, no steam.

3. Place the white wax paper on your work surface. Fold it in half so it measures 7 x 4½ inches (17.8 x 11.4 cm). Crease it with a bone folder. Fold it in half again so it measures 3½ x 4½ inches (8.9 x 11.4 cm), and crease with a bone folder again.

4. Nest the signature into the folded wax paper cover. Pick up the newly formed pamphlet and turn it upside down so the top edge is at the bottom. Jog the pamphlet so the top edges (the folded edge of the wax paper cover) are aligned.

5. With a pencil, mark the wax paper along the fore and bottom edges of the signature (A). Remove the wax paper cover from the pamphlet and use a paper cutter to trim the fore and bottom edges to size.

6. Place the sheet of craft paper on top of a heat-safe worktable (a wooden surface, for example). Hold the wax paper cover so the front panel is facing you. Unfold it by pulling the back cover to the left (B). Set it on the table and fold the top panel up (C).

7. Arrange the dried petals or leaves on the bottom-right panel.

8. Fold the top edge of the wax paper cover down to meet the bottom edge, using care not to disturb the flower arrangement (D).

9. Be sure all edges are aligned. Press the heated iron over the front and back panels of the wax paper to seal the flowers between the two layers. Once the layers are sealed (after about 10 seconds), turn the iron off and set it aside to cool.

PUNCH THE HOLES

10. Refold the wax paper cover along the spine to create a front and back cover; the pressed violet is on the front. Place the wax paper cover around the signature.

11. Create a punch guide using Template 1. Nest the punch guide inside the pamphlet and place the pamphlet in the gutter of an open phonebook. Gently punch the holes with the awl.

finished dimensions

3 x 4 x ⅛ inches (7.6 x 10.2 x 0.3 cm)

stitch used

Running stitch (page 20)

what you need

Basic Bookmaking Toolkit (page 13)

7 sheets of text-weight paper; 5¾ x 4 inches (14.6 x 10.2 cm)

Pressing iron

1 sheet of white wax paper; 7 x 9 inches (17.8 x 22.9 cm)

1 sheet of craft paper, 8 x 10 inches (20.3 x 25.4 cm)

Dried petals or leaves

2 16-inch (40.6 cm) lengths of embroidery floss, color(s) of your choice

Corner rounder (optional)

Book press or other weights (optional)

fig. A

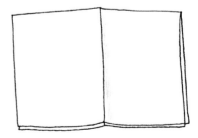

fig. B

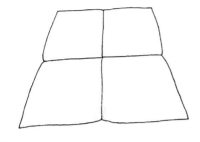

fig. C

fig. D

fig. E

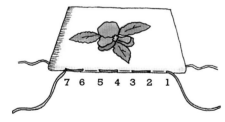

fig. F

fig. G

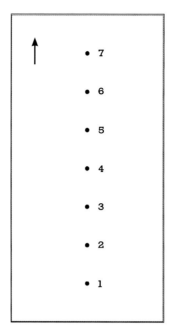

template 1
2 x 4 inches (5.1 x 10.2 cm)

Enlarge template by 20%

ASSEMBLE THE BOOK

12. With the needle and one of the lengths of embroidery floss, enter into the outside of the sewing station 1. Pull the floss into the center of the pamphlet and leave 6 inches (15.2 cm) of loose floss on the outside of the cover.

13. Go through station 2 and out the cover.

14. Enter into station 3 from the outside and pull the floss to the inside of the pamphlet. Continue weaving in and out of the stations with a running stitch. Once you pull the floss through sewing station 7, remove the needle from the floss. Do not trim the floss (E).

15. Thread the needle with the remaining length of floss and open the pamphlet. Enter the needle into the sewing station 1 from inside and pull the thread to the outside of the pamphlet. Leave 6 inches (15.2 cm) of loose floss on the inside of the cover. Continue to weave in and out of the stations with a running stitch. Once you pull the floss through sewing station 7, slide the needle from the floss (F).

16. Finish the binding by tying the loose threads located at the top and bottom of the spine with a square knot (page 28) (G). Use scissors to trim each set of threads to 4 inches (10.2 cm).

17. Place the pamphlet in a book press or under a stack of heavy books or weights to flatten if needed.

OPTIONAL: Use a corner rounder to round the pamphlets' two fore edge corners.

FLOWER PRESSING

Choose flowers that are fresh and well hydrated to help retain the color and shape of the petals.

When pressing whole flowers, select ones that are thin and flat. If the center of the flower is bulky and thick, consider detaching the petals from the core of the flower and pressing the petals individually.

Arrange the petals or flowers between the pages of a press or an old book so none of the petals overlap.

Drying time depends on the thickness of the flower and the amount of heat and moisture in the environment. Petals may be removed from the press when they are completely dried, which may take from one to several weeks. When dried, they will appear firm and no longer cold to the touch.

LEATHER
BOOKS

OLD TIME REVIVAL

Built with the basics, this leather-bound journal is a classic that uses an extra interior leather spine for durability.

finished dimensions

5 x 5¾ x 1½ inches (12.7 x 14.6 x 3.8 cm)

stitches used

Long stitch (page 21), gathering stitch (page 24)

what you need

Basic Bookmaking Toolkit (page 13)

Bookbinding thread, 65 inches (165 cm); 12 inches (30 cm) for closure

56 sheets of writing paper, 8½ x 5⁷⁄₁₆ inches (21.6 x 13.8 cm)

4 sheets of handmade paper with deckled edges, 8⅞ x 5½ inches (22.5 x 14 cm)

1 sheet of cardstock, 8½ x 11 inches (21.6 x 27.9 cm)

2 to 4 ounces leather, 1 x 5¾ inches (2.5 x 14.6 cm)

¹⁄₁₆-inch (1.6 mm) leather punch

2 to 4 ounces leather for the cover, 14 x 5¾ inches (35.6 x 14.6 cm)

2 to 4 ounces leather strip, 18 x ½ inches (45.7 x 1.3 cm)

MAKE THE TEXT BLOCK

1. Divide the writing paper into seven stacks of eight sheets. With your bone folder, fold each stack into a signature measuring 4¼ x 5⁷⁄₁₆ inches (10.8 x 13.8 cm). Arrange the seven signatures into a text block and set aside.

2. Place a sheet of handmade paper on your work surface in the horizontal position. Position a signature on the right side of the handmade paper so the right fore edges of the signature and handmade paper align. Fold the left side of the handmade paper over the top of the signature to meet the right edges. Crease the fold with a bone folder. Repeat these steps for the remaining three handmade sheets.

3. Arrange the four wrapped signatures within the text block by alternating the wrapped signatures with unwrapped ones. The wrapped signatures will be positioned first, third, fifth, and seventh in the text block (A).

TIP: For a rustic look, choose handmade paper that has deckled top and left-hand edges and position the deckle along the top and left-hand edges of the four sheets, then wrap them around the signatures.

PUNCH HOLES IN THE SIGNATURES

4. Use the sheet of cardstock to create a punch template (see page 17) from Template 1.

5. Nest the punch template inside each signature and use an awl to punch all stations. After each signature is punched, arrange them into a text block and set them aside.

fig. A

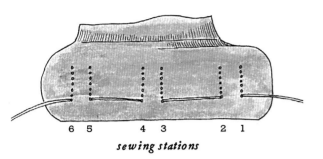

fig. B

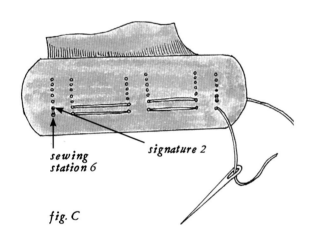

fig. C

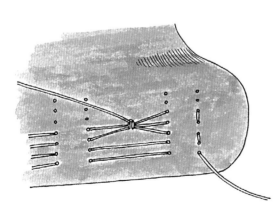

fig. D

sewing stations

sewing station 6

signature 2

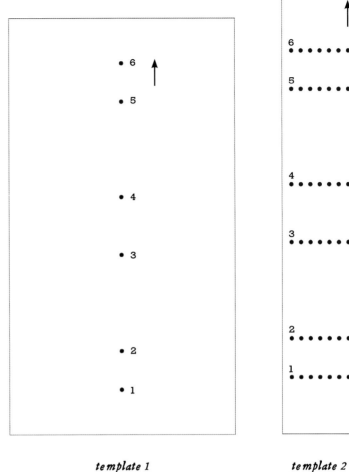

template 1
3 x 5⁷⁄₁₆ inches
(7.6 x 13.8 cm)

template 2
1 x 5¾ inches
(2.5 x 14.6 cm)

PREPARE THE SPINE

6. Use the remaining cardstock to create a template from Template 2.

7. Place the 1 x 5¾-inch (2.5 x 14.6 cm) leather piece on your work surface with the front side facing up. Align the spine template on the top of the leather. Use a pencil or awl to mark the template holes onto the leather.

8. Punch the holes into the leather using a ¹⁄₁₆-inch (1.6 mm) leather punch.

PREPARE THE COVER

9. Place the large leather piece (the cover) in a horizontal position on your work surface so the back side is facing up.

10. Use a pencil to mark 4⅝ inches (11.8 cm) from the left straight edge of the leather. Mark both the top and bottom edges of the leather. Align a metal ruler to the marks and draw a straight line to link them.

11. Align the leather spine, front side facing up, to the right of the line. Position the spine so the top and bottom edges align with those of the cover. Hold the spine securely to the cover and use an awl or pencil to mark the holes of the spine onto the cover.

12. Set the spine aside. Use the leather punch to punch the holes in the cover. You may need to roll the leather to reach the interior holes.

13. Return the spine, front side facing up, on the inside of the cover and align the holes of both pieces.

ASSEMBLE THE BOOK

14. Prepare the text block for binding. Make certain all signatures are in order. Position the cover and spine so the inside is facing up and the fore edge of the top cover is facing you. Pull the bottom signature from the text block and place it within the cover aligned to sewing station 1 of the spine.

15. Signature 1: Lift the front edge of the cover and enter the threaded needle into sewing station 1 of the leather, draw it through the spine, and into the interior of the signature. Leave a tail of 6 inches (15.2 cm) on the outside of the spine.

16. Continue sewing with a continuous long stitch through all three layers (signature, spine, and cover) until you arrive on the outside of the spine on sewing station 6 (B).

17. Signature 2: Enter into the closest hole in the next row on the outside of the leather (sewing station 6). This will be a direct link—no kettle stitches. Pull a signature from the bottom of the stack and place it within the cover. Draw the needle into the signature and pull the thread taut. Continue sewing the remaining signatures using this long stitch pattern (C).

18. Consider adding gathering stitches while sewing signature 5 by gathering the two previous signatures' threads between stations 2 and 3 and 4 and 5 (D).

19. After the last signature is attached with the long stitch, weave the threaded needle in and out of the top stations of the cover only near the head of the spine to fill in the threadless gaps between stations (E).

20. Once all gaps are filled, enter into the nearest signature and tie off (see Tying Off the Binding, page 27). Trim the thread ends to ¼ inch (6 mm).

21. Thread the remaining tail onto the needle and repeat step 19 at the other end of the spine.

ATTACH THE CLOSURE

22. Place the long leather strip on your work surface. Choose one end and align it to the ruler. Mark points in the center of the strip ¼, ½, and ¾ inch (6 mm, 1.3 cm, and 1.9 cm) from the end of the leather. Use the leather punch to punch the marks.

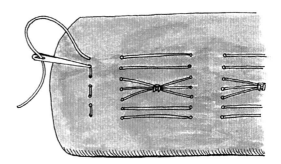

fig. E

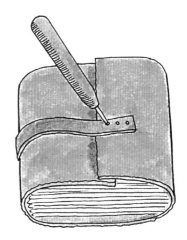

fig. F

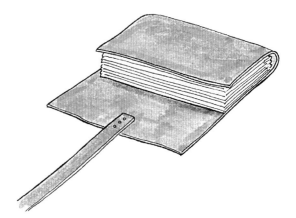

fig. G

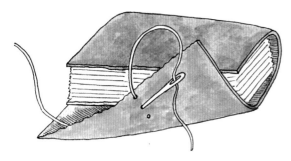

fig. H

fig. I

23. Place the journal on your work surface with the cover closed. Place the punched end of the strip in the center of the wraparound leather portion of the cover. Position the strip so the first hole is ¼ inch (6 mm) from the edge of the wraparound panel. Use a pencil or awl to mark the three holes of the strip onto the cover (F).

24. Punch the holes in the cover using the leather punch.

25. Thread a needle with 12 inches (30.5 cm) of binder's thread.

26. Open the wraparound panel and position it so the edge is facing you. Place the leather strip's back side faceup so the holes align with the holes in the cover (G).

27. Enter the needle into the nearest hole on the backside of the strip. Pull it through to the front of the cover.

28. Gently pull both ends of the thread until they're even.

29. With the needle, continue into the second hole on the outside of the cover and pull through to the inside of the strip (H).

30. Remove the needle and attach it to the other end of the thread.

31. Enter the needle into the second hole on the inside of the strip and pull to the outside of the cover (I).

32. Enter into the third hole in the cover from the outside, and pull to the inside of the strip.

33. Pull both threads so they are taut. Remove the needle and tie off the thread with a square knot (J).

34. Trim the threads to 1/4 inch (6 mm).

35. Fasten the journal by wrapping the leather strip twice around the spine and then tucking the end beneath both strips on the front of the cover.

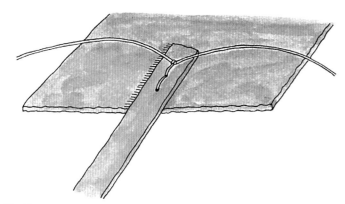

fig. J

LITTLE TRAVELER

By air, rail, or road, this notebook is a durable companion in a ready-to-go size: fit for your pocket, twined and tasseled for your twiddling thumbs.

finished dimensions

2¾ x 4 x ¾ inches (7 x 10.2 x 1.9 cm)

stitch used

Pamphlet stitch (page 20)

what you need

Basic Bookmaking Toolkit (page 13)

Bookbinding thread, 2 lengths of 38 inches (97 cm)

1 sheet of cardstock, 8½ x 11 inches (21.6 x 27.9 cm)

2 to 4 ounces leather, 7 x 4 inches (17.8 x 10.2 cm)

¹⁄₁₆- and ⅛-inch (1.6 and 3 mm) hole punch

32 sheets of text-weight paper, 5 x 3½ inches (12.7 x 8.9 cm)

2 decorative end sheets, 3 x 3½ inches (7.6 x 8.9 cm)

Corner rounder (optional)

Line 24 heavy-duty snap

Snap setter

MAKE THE COVER

1. Create a cover guide on cardstock using Template 1.

2. With an awl, trace around the outside of the cover guide on the piece of leather and mark the holes.

3. Cut the leather along the traced line using the scissors.

4. Punch the marked holes on the leather using the hole punches. Punch the three spine holes with the ¹⁄₁₆-inch (1.6 mm) punch and the snap holes with the ⅛-inch (3 mm) punch.

MAKE THE SIGNATURES

5. Divide the text-weight paper into eight stacks of four sheets each. Fold each stack into a signature that measures 2½ x 3½ inches (6.4 x 8.9 cm) using the bone folder.

6. Nest four signatures into a single signature. Nest the remaining four signatures the same way. You will now have two large signatures (A).

ADD THE END SHEETS

7. Align the fore edges of the end sheets to the fore edges of the first and last pages in the text block. Wrap them around the spine of the signatures and crease them with the bone folder.

fig. A

fig. B

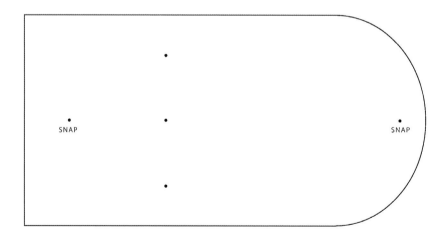

template 1
7¾ x 4 inches (19.7 x 10.2 cm)

Enlarge template by 45%

PUNCH THE HOLES

8. Use the remaining card stock to create a punch guide from Template 2.

fig. C

template 2
2 x 3½ inches (5.1 x 8.9 cm)

Enlarge template by 30%

9. Nest the punch guide inside the first signature, and place the signature in the gutter of an open phone book. Punch the holes with the awl (C). Repeat for the second signature.

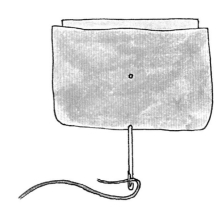

fig. D

ASSEMBLE THE BOOK

10. Double-thread two needles (see page 18). Place the leather on your work surface with the back side facing up. Place the front signature along the spine holes in the leather so the sewing stations align.

11. Draw one threaded needle from the outside of the center sewing station (station 1) on the cover through the center sewing station of the first signature into the inside of the signature (D).

12. Pull the needle until 6 inches (15.2 cm) of thread remain on the outside of the cover.

13. Enter through the top sewing station (station 2) and pull the needle through to the outside of the cover (E) Set the needle down.

14. Place the second signature inside the leather behind the front signature. Draw the second threaded needle from the outside of the center sewing station (station 1) on the cover to the center sewing station inside the second signature.

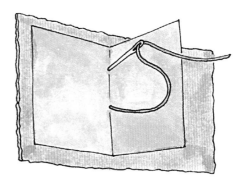

fig. E

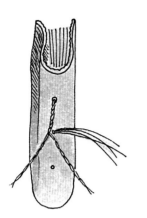

fig. F

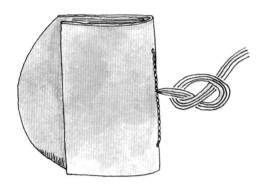

fig. G

15. Like before, pull the needle until 6 inches (15.2 cm) of thread remain on the outside of the cover.

16. Again enter through the top sewing station and pull the needle through to the outside of the cover.

17. Hold the book vertically with the spine facing you. Hold both threads apart from one another and simultaneously begin to twist the threads clockwise. As the threads become twisted, begin to wrap them around each other in a counterclockwise direction. This continuous motion will twine the threads together. Continue twining the threads tightly until you reach the bottom sewing station. Keep the loose ends of the thread that hang from the center sewing station off to one side of the twine (F).

18. Push both needles, one at a time, through the bottom sewing station (station 3). One of the threads will enter into the bottom sewing station on the front signature, and the other will enter through the same station on the back signature.

19. Draw both needles through the center sewing station in each signature and pull them both to the outside of the cover. Be sure to direct them to the side of the twine that is opposite the thread's tail ends from earlier.

20. Pull all threads taut, making certain there is no slack between the signatures and the cover.

21. Hold the cover with one hand and the threads with the other. Make a loop knot (page 28) and press the knot tightly to the spine (G).

22. Make a tassel by trimming all threads to 1 inch (2.5 cm) (H).

OPTIONAL: Using a corner rounder, round the two corners of the cover's fore edge.

SET THE SNAP

23. Set the snap as directed for your snap setter.

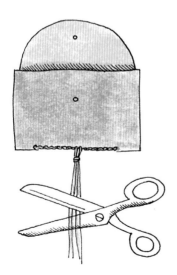

fig. H

HANGING LEDGER

Account for your dreams, your wishes, and the mundane tasks on your to-do list.

MAKE THE TEXT BLOCK

1. Arrange all text-weight sheets into one stack.

2. Place one end sheet on the top of the stack and the other on the bottom.

MAKE THE TIE

3. Knot the 4 lengths of binder's thread with a slip knot and use your awl to securely fasten the knotted end of the ties to a wooden board.

4. Divide the binder's thread into two groups of two. Twine the threads together (see figure F on page 106) and finish with a slip knot (A). Set aside until you are ready to assemble the cover.

DRILL THE HOLES

5. Jog the text block so all edges are flush.

6. Secure the text block tightly with a rubber band 1½ inches (3.8 cm) from the top edge.

7. Use cardstock to create a punch guide from Template 1. Align it to the top edge of the text block and secure it beneath the rubber band. Secure the top edge of the text block and guide with a second rubber band ½ inch (1.3 cm) from the top. Check to make sure all edges of the text block are flush.

finished dimensions

4 x 9 x 1 inches (10.2 x 22.9 x 2.5 cm)

stitch used

Japanese stab binding (page 110)

what you need

Basic Bookmaking Toolkit (page 13)

128 sheets of text-weight paper (or enough sheets to make a ¾-inch [1.9 cm] stack, including end sheets), 4 x 8½ inches (10.2 x 21.6 cm)

2 decorative end sheets, 4 x 8½ inches (10.2 x 21.6 cm)

4 lengths of binder's thread, 25 inches (63.5 cm) each

Cardstock

Wooden board, at least 5 x 10 inches (12.7 x 25.4 cm)

2 rubber bands, 2½ x ¼ inches (6.4 x 0.6 cm)

Dust mask

Handheld drill with 5/64-inch (2 mm) wood bit

Leather, 4 x 22 inches (10.2 x 55.9 cm)

1/16-inch (1.6 mm) leather punch

2 lengths of binder's thread, 60 inches (152.4 cm) each

Line 24 heavy-duty snap

Snap setter

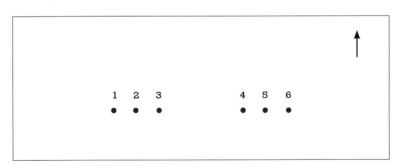

template 1
7¾ x 4 inches (19.7 x 10.2 cm)

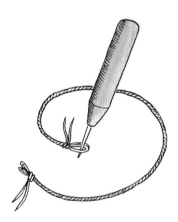

fig. A

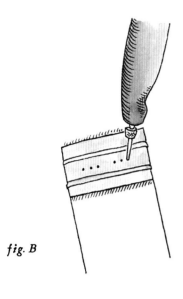

fig. B

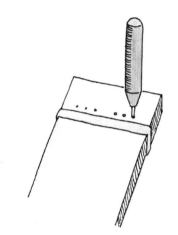

fig. C

fig. D

8. Put on your dust mask. Place the text block on a wooden board and have your drill ready to use.

9. Hold the text block securely with one hand. With the other hand, drill a straight hole through the guide and text block on each of the marked holes. Be certain to hold the drill at a 90° angle so the holes will be straight through from front to back (B).

10. Take off your mask and remove the top rubber band and guide from the text block. Brush away any paper dust.

MAKE THE COVER

11. Wrap the leather cover around the text block by aligning one edge of the leather cover to the bottom edge of the text block front.

12. Turn the cover and text block over, and place it on your worktable so the back side of the ledger is faceup.

13. Lift the back leather cover and fold it open so the back of the text block is showing.

14. With an awl, press through each of the holes in the text block to leave a mark on the leather below. Set the text block aside.

15. Punch the marked holes on the leather using a ¹⁄₁₆-inch (1.6 mm) leather punch.

16. Again wrap the leather around the text block as in step 11. This time, lift the front leather cover and fold it open so the top of the text block is showing.

17. Repeat steps 14 and 15 (C) to mark the holes on the back of the leather cover.

ASSEMBLE THE BOOK

18. Place the leather cover on the text block and align the holes.

19. Lift the front cover and slip the twined tie (from step 4) between the cover and spine of the text block. Pull the ends so the tie is centered. Leave the ends loose until the stab binding is complete (D).

20. Single-thread a needle with two 60-inch (152.4 cm) lengths of binder's thread.

21. To start, temporarily lift the text block away from the back cover. Guide the needle and thread it through the back of station 3 on the text block only. Return the text block to the cover and guide the needle out the matching hole on the front cover. Pull until just 4 inches (10.2 cm) of loose thread remains between the text block and the back cover (E).

22. Close the back cover. Bring the thread around the spine and sew it through station 3 from the back and out the front cover again (F). This creates the first vertical stitch, which runs from station 3 on the front to station 3 on the back.

23. Pull the thread and enter into station 2 from the front. This will create a horizontal stitch between station 3 and station 2 on the front side of the ledger. Go out the back cover. Bring the thread up and around the spine to the front side again, through station 2 again, and out the back cover, creating another vertical stitch, this time between station 2 on the back and station 2 on the front (G).

24. Pull the thread and enter into station 1, creating a horizontal stitch between stations 2 and 1 on the back side of the ledger (H). Go through station 1 and out the front side (I). Bring the thread up and around the spine and sew through station 1 from the back side a second time (J), and out the front cover again, making a vertical stitch between station 1 on the front to station 1 on the back.

25. Bring the thread around the outer edge of the ledger, sewing it into station 1 from the back, and out the front cover. This creates a long horizontal stitch that wraps all the way around the side (K).

26. Enter into station 2 from the front and then out the back cover. This will create a horizontal stitch between stations 1 and 2 on the front side.

27. Enter into station 3 from the back and then out the front cover, creating a horizontal stitch between stations 2 and 3 on the back.

28. Enter into station 4 from the front and then out the back cover, making a long horizontal stitch across the space between stations 3 and 4 on the front side. Bring the thread around the spine back to the front and into station 4, creating a vertical stitch.

29. Enter into station 5 from the front and out the back cover to create the vertical stitch between stations 4 and 5 on the front side. Bring the thread around the spine to the back, into station 5 and out the front cover to make the vertical stitch.

30. Enter into station 6 from the front and out the back cover. This will create a horizontal stitch between stations 5 and 6 on the front. Bring the thread around the spine to the back and into station 6, then out the back cover for your vertical stitch.

31. Bring the thread around the outer edge of the text block as you did earlier, and into station 6 through the front cover.

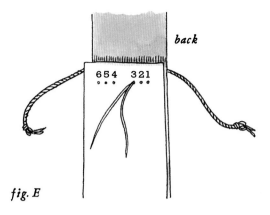

fig. E

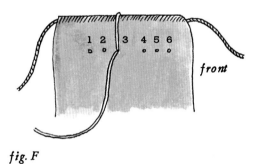

fig. F

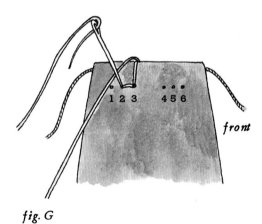

fig. G

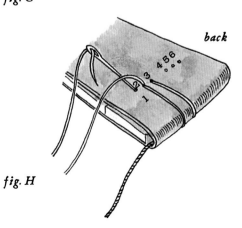

fig. H

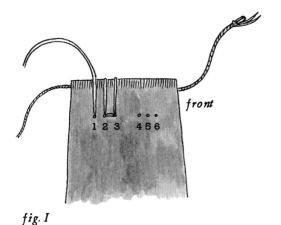

fig. I

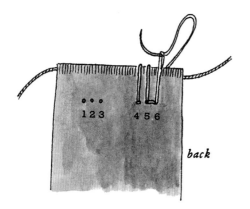

fig. J

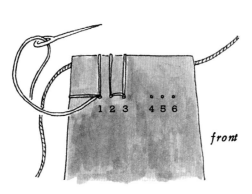

fig. K

32. Enter into station 5 from the back and pull the thread out the front cover. This will give you your horizontal stitch between stations 6 and 5 on the ledger's back side.

33. Enter into station 4 from the front and guide the thread through the back cover. Reenter the same station and pull the thread between the back cover and the text block to the inside, meeting the loose end of the other thread.

34. Pull both threads taut and tie a square knot (page 28). With a pair of scissors, trim the excess thread to ½ inch (1.3 cm).

35. Pull both ends of the twined tie that runs the length of the spine inside until they are centered with the ledger. Untie both of the slipknots from the ends. Gather all of the thread ends together and tie them securely in a loop knot (page 28) 1 inch (2.5 cm) from the end. With a pair of scissors, trim the threads to 1 inch (2.5 cm).

SET THE SNAP

36. On the bottom edge of the inner back cover, use a pencil to mark the snap position 1 inch (2.5 cm) from the bottom and 2 inches (5.1 cm) from either side.

37. With the leather punch, punch a hole through the mark.

38. To find the placement of the snap on the front cover, insert the snap top in the punched hole. Wrap the long end of the back cover over the top (as if the ledger is closed). Press the snap firmly into the front cover to mark the position of the second hole.

39. With your leather punch, punch a hole through the mark.

40. Set the snap according to the manufacturer's instructions.

STAR-STITCHED

Weave this decorative element into the cover of your book. (See page 115.)

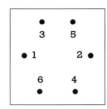

template 1
1 x 1 inch (2.5 x 2.5 cm)

1. Make a punch guide on the cardstock from Template 1.

2. Position the guide on the material you've chosen to stitch on.

3. Use an awl to lightly mark the holes from the guide onto the material (A).

4. Use an awl or hole punch to make holes where the marks are.

5. Single-thread the needle and follow the stitching pattern below.

NOTE: Each hole will be sewn through twice so there will be a double row of threads between each pair of holes.

6. Begin sewing by first entering the needle into the back side of station 1 (B).

7. Pull the thread to the front of the material until you have a tail of 3 inches on the back side of the material. Enter sewing station 2 and pull thread to the back of the material. Again, enter station 1 and pull the thread to station 2 and to the back (C).

8. Enter sewing station 3 and pull the thread to the front of the material. Guide the needle over the first thread and under the second thread (D).

stitches used

Decorative, instructed below

what you need

Basic Bookmaking Toolkit (page 13)

Bookbinding thread, 18 inches (116 cm)

Awl or hole punch

Cardstock

fig. A

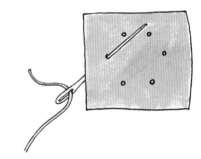

fig. B

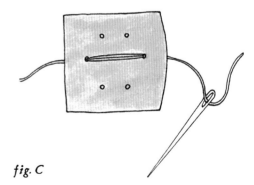

fig. C

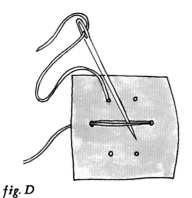

fig. D

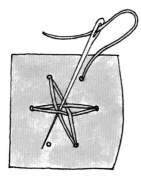

fig. E

fig. F

fig. G

9. Enter into sewing station 4 and pull thread to the back.

10. Again enter station 3 and pull thread to the front of the material. Guide the needle under the first thread and over the second thread (E).

11. Enter into sewing station 4.

12. Enter into station 5 and pull thread to the front.

13. Guide the needle over the two nearest intersecting threads and under the two farthest intersecting threads (F).

14. Enter into station 6 and pull thread to the back.

15. Again, enter into station 5 and pull thread to the front. Guide the needle under the nearest intersecting two threads and over the farthest two intersecting threads (G).

16. Enter into sewing station 6 and pull thread to the back of the material. You have now completed the star stitch.

17. Tie off (page 27) the tails on the backside and trim them to ⅛ inch.

BOTANICAL PRESS

This petite, transportable press is used to gather
and preserve botanical specimens.

MAKE THE TEXT BLOCK

1. Using a bone folder, fold the sheets of handmade paper so they measure 4⅜ x 5¼ inches (11.1 x 13.3 cm).

2. Nest the sheets into four signatures of three sheets each.

3. Insert a sheet of cardboard into the center of each signature. With a bone folder, gently form the spine of each signature around the edge of the cardboard. The cardboard helps to keep the pages flat.

4. Remove the cardboard sheets from the signatures.

PUNCH SEWING STATIONS

5. Make a cardstock punch guide using Template 1. Place the signatures one at a time in the gutter of an open phonebook, nest the punch guide (page 18) into the signature, and use an awl to punch the sewing binding.

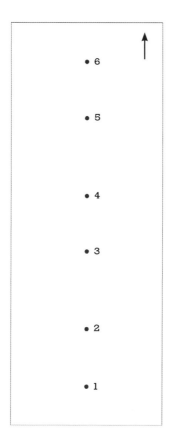

template 1
2 x 5¼ inches (5.1 x 13.3 cm)

Enlarge template by 20%

finished dimensions

4¾ x 5½ x 1¼ inches (12 x 14 x 4.4 cm)

stitches used

Running stitch (page 20), true kettle stitch (page 24)

what you need

Basic Bookmaking Toolkit (page 13)

Bookbinding thread, 30 inches (76 cm)

12 sheets of handmade 300g paper, 8¾ x 5¼ inches (22.2 x 5.25 cm)

4 sheets of cardboard, 4¼ x 5¼ x ⅛ inches (10.8 x 13.3 x 0.3 cm) each

2 wooden boards for the cover, 4½ x 5½ x ³⁄₁₆ inches (11.4 x 14 x 0.5 cm) (horizontal grain)

Cardstock

3-4 ounce leather wrap, 14¾ x 3½ inches (37.5 x 8.9 cm)

¹⁄₁₆-inch (1.6 mm) leather punch

Wood scrap board, 6 x 7 inches (15.2 x 17.8 cm) minimum

Dust mask

Handheld drill with ¹⁄₁₆-inch (1.6 mm) wood bit

Leather strip for the tie, ½ x 31 inches (1.3 x 78.7 cm)

fig. A

fig. B

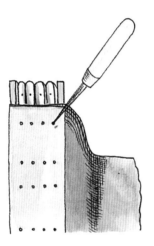

fig. C

fig. D

6. Return the cardboard sheets to the interior of the signatures and place the wooden covers on the front and back of the text block. Jog the book along the spine so all layers are flush.

7. Align the fore edge of the leather wrap to the fore edge of the front wooden cover and wrap the leather tightly around the spine, coming back to the front cover and overlapping the leather on the front cover (A) (B).

8. Hold the entire book tightly so the signatures are compressed as if bound. Align Template 2 to the spine so the holes align to the fold of the signatures.

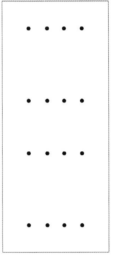

template 2
1½ x 3½ inches (3.8 x 8.9 cm)

Enlarge template by 25%

9. With an awl, mark the sewing stations on the leather (C).

10. Remove the leather from the book and punch the marked holes with the leather punch.

DRILL HOLES IN THE WOODEN COVERS

11. Gather the text block and wooden covers. Gently jog the book along the spine so the signatures are flush with the cover edges.

12. Center the spine of the text block within the spine edge of the covers.

13. With a pencil, mark the front and back covers ¼ inch (6 mm) from the edges of the boards in alignment with both the top and bottom sewing stations (four marks total, two on each cover).

14. Place one of the wooden covers on the scrap wood. Put on a dust mask. Drill holes through the cover where you marked, being careful to hold the drill at a 90° angle to ensure straight holes. Repeat for the other cover (D).

ASSEMBLE THE BOOK

15. Gather the text block and leather wrap. Align the holes of the signatures with the holes on the leather. (The wooden covers may be set aside until the binding of the text block is complete.)

NOTE: The cardboard sheets will remain floating inside the signatures while the book is bound. Be sure to leave them in place so the thickness of the cardboard will be accounted for in the stitching. The boards may be temporarily moved to access the holes with the needle in each signature, but should be immediately replaced after the holes are accessed.

16. Starting with sewing station 1 in the bottom signature, push the needle into the inside of the signature.

17. Pull the thread until 8 inches (20.3 cm) of loose thread remains on the outside. Push the needle through sewing station 2 from the inside to the outside (E).

18. Continue sewing with the running stitch method, using true kettle stitches at the far left and right sewing stations (1 and 6) (F).

19. When you're finished, attach the wooden covers using the method for even-numbered signatures (page 26).

ATTACH THE TIE

20. Punch a hole with your awl ¼ inch (6 mm) from one end of the leather strip. Punch a second hole ¼ inch (6 mm) from the first hole.

21. Align the holes on the tie to the top of the wraparound edge of the leather cover so the second hole is ¼ inch (6 mm) from the edge. Using your awl, mark the position of the tie holes on the leather cover. Punch the marked holes with the awl (G).

22. With a needle and 12 inches (30.5 cm) of binder's thread, sew the tie to the leather cover, starting on the inside of the cover. Enter through one of the holes in the tie and pull the thread through the cover hole to the outside of the cover. Enter into the second hole on the cover and pull the thread through to the inside of the tie. Repeat once (H).

23. Tie off the thread on the inside with a double knot. Trim the threads to ¼ inch (6 mm).

24. Wrap the tie around the bound press twice, and secure it by tucking the end beneath both ties.

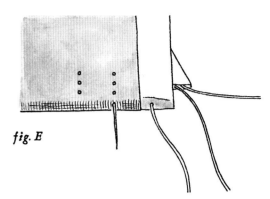

fig. E

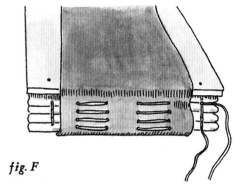

fig. F

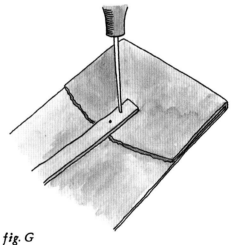

fig. G

fig. H

LEATHER PHOTO ALBUM

Revive your used photo album with a
protective leather cover and ornamental stitching.

PREPARE THE SPINE

1. Determine the height of the leather spine by measuring the height of the text block and adding ¼ inch (6 mm). Determine the width of the leather spine piece by aligning the right edge of the leather piece ¼ inch (6 mm) to the right of the top cover's post bindings.

2. Hold the leather securely near the edge and wrap it around the text block spine to ¼ inch (6 mm) beyond the post bindings on the back page. Use a pencil to mark this spot on the leather (A). Place the leather on your work surface and use scissors to trim it to the marked width. Measure the spine's height on the leather, mark it, and trim it to size.

3. Wrap the leather spine around the spine of the text block as in step 1. With your pencil, feel for the center of the metal posts below the leather. Mark the leather where the center of the top and bottom of the posts are positioned. There should be four marks total.

4. Use the ⅛-inch leather punch to punch holes through the four marks.

5. Integrate the leather spine into the text block. Start by securing the album pages with two rubber bands—one vertical, one horizontal.

6. Unscrew the top metal post and carefully take it out. Insert the post into the correlating spine hole and into the back of the text block and out the top hole. Guide the post into the front leather hole and twist the metal cap onto the post to close.

7. Repeat step 6 for the bottom metal post (B).

PREPARE THE COVER

8. Determine the height of the leather cover by measuring the height of the text block and adding ¼ inch (6 mm). Use scissors to cut your piece of leather to this height. The width is yet to be determined.

9. Begin determining the width of the cover by first measuring the width from the fore edge of the first page of the text block to the left edge of the leather spine. Multiply this measurement by two. Record this number.

10. Measure the depth of the text block (photo pages only) and multiply that by two. Record this number.

11. Again, measure the width of the text block (photo pages only). Divide this number in half. Record this number.

12. Add all recorded measurements. This is the width of your leather cover.

13. Mark the leather cover with the determined measurements using a straight edge ruler and cut it to size with scissors.

finished dimensions

Approximately 6 x 6½ x 2 inches (15 x 16.5 x 5.1 cm)

stitches used

Decorative stitching

what you need

Basic Bookmaking Toolkit (page 13)

Bookbinding thread, 56 inches (142 cm)

Leather spine strip, to be determined by size of text block

Cover leather, to be determined by size of text block

Recycled text block from a 4 x 6-inch (10 x 15-cm) post bound photo album (single panel), removed from original cover with metal post screws and spacers intact.

1/16-, 1/18-, and ¼-inch (1.6-, 1.5-, and 6.3-mm) leather punch

Heavy-duty line, 32 snap

Snap setter

fig. A

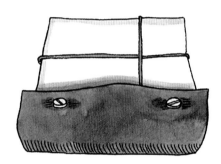

fig. B

OPTIONAL: Position the left edge of the cover along the raw, uneven edge of the leather (if it has one) to give the wraparound cover a wild, rustic look.

PUNCH HOLES IN THE LEATHER SPINE

14. Create a spine guide on cardstock using Template 1. The measurements provided for the template should work for any 4 x 6 album, even though the cover and spine measurements may vary a little, depending upon the dimensions of the text block.

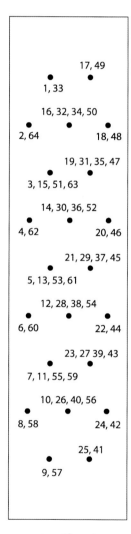

template 1
1¼ x 5¼ inches (3.2 x 13.3 cm)

15. Hold the text block upright with the spine facing you. Center the punch template on the spine.

16. With an awl or pencil, mark the hole positions through the template onto the leather cover (C).

17. Remove the leather spine from the text block, one metal post at a time.

18. Place the leather spine faceup on your work surface. With a ⅛-inch (1.6 mm) leather punch, punch the marked holes in the leather.

19. Reattach the leather spine to the text block, one metal post at a time.

PUNCH HOLES IN THE LEATHER COVER

20. Place the leather cover, back side up, on your work surface. Place the text block on the leather.

21. Align the fore edge of the leather cover to the fore edge of the text block and apply pressure to hold the edges together. Pull the back part of the cover until the leather is firmly wrapped around the spine of the text block.

22. Make sure the top and bottom edges of the leather spine piece are aligned to the top and bottom edges of the leather cover. Place the album on the work surface so it is faceup.

23. With a pencil, make marks on the inside of the leather cover near the four corners of the leather spine (D).

24. Unwrap the cover. Carefully remove the leather spine from the text block.

25. Place the cover, back side up, on the table. Position the leather spine, also back side up, so it is centered between the pencil marks, and the top and bottom edges of the spine and cover are aligned.

26. Use a pencil to mark the hole positions through the spine onto the leather cover. Set the spine aside.

27. Use the ¹⁄₁₆-inch (1.6 mm) punch to make holes in the cover.

ASSEMBLE THE ALBUM

28. Place the leather cover back side up on your work surface. Place the leather spine, back side up, on top of the cover. Align the holes in the spine to the holes in the cover.

29. To begin, enter the single-threaded needle into sewing station 1 (the top left hole) through the spine and cover piece. Pull the thread to the outside of the cover, leaving a 2-inch (5.1 cm) tail on the inside of the spine. Using the Template 1 as a sewing guide, follow the numbers in chronological order as you stitch the spine and cover together. As you follow the numbers, you will create a weaving pattern with the thread moving from the inside to the outside of the spine. At the final stitch (sewing station 65),

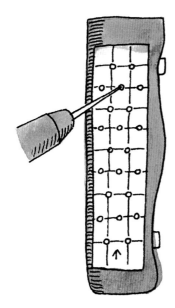

fig. C

fig. D

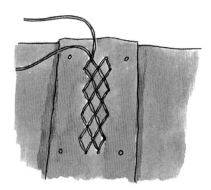

fig. E

the needle and thread should be inside the spine. Pull the needle off the thread, pull both the tails taut, and tie them off with a square knot (page 28). Trim the ends to ¼ inch (6 mm) (E).

30. Attach the stitched cover to the text block by carefully removing one of the text block posts. Attach to the correlating spine holes and fasten the cap on the post. Remove the rubber bands from the text block. Carefully remove the remaining text block post. Attach to the correlating spine holes and fasten the cap on the post.

SET THE SNAP

31. Wrap the cover firmly around the text block.

32. On the front flap edge, determine the center point and mark it with a pencil (F).

33. Measure ½ inch (1.3 cm) in (i.e., toward the fore edge) from the center mark you made at the end of the leather and punch a hole with the ⅛-inch (3 mm) hole punch. Insert and set the top snap pieces according to the snap setter's directions.

34. Position the front cover flap in its closed position. Press the back of the snap firmly into the underlying leather to make a slight indentation. This will be the placement for the bottom half of the snap.

35. Use the ⅛ inch hole punch to punch a hole in the center of the indentation. Insert the bottom snap pieces and set the snap.

fig. F

FIELD JOURNAL

The leather spine on this journal will strengthen the binding, so go ahead and pack it up for your outing. You don't want to miss anything.

finished dimensions

4 x 6 x 1 inches (10.2 x 15.2 x 2.5 cm)

stitches used

Running stitch (page 20), true kettle stitch (page 24), gathering stitch (optional)

what you need

Basic Bookmaking Toolkit (page 13)

Vintage book cover (text block removed), approximately 4 x 6 inches (10.2 x 15.2 cm) when closed, or 2 binder's boards, 4 x 6 x ³⁄₁₆ inches (10.2 x 15.2 x 0.5 cm), plus bookbinding paper or cloth to cover

¹⁄₁₆ inch (1.6 mm) leather punch

Utility knife (optional)

54 sheets of 70 lb. writing paper, 8½ x 11 inches (21.6 x 27.9 cm)

2 sheets of decorative paper, 8½ x 11 inches (21.6 x 27.9 cm)

4 to 5 ounces (113.4 to 141.8 g) of leather, ⁷⁄₈ x 4 inches (2.2 x 10.2 cm)

³⁄₃₂-inch (2.3 mm) hole punch

1 sheet of cardstock, 8½ x 11 inches (21.6 x 27.9 cm)

Book press or weights

PREPARE THE COVER

The cover can be salvaged from a 4 x 6-inch (10.2 x 15.2 cm) vintage book, or cut from binder's board and covered with your choice of cloth or paper (see page 19, Deconstructing a Book).

Option 1: Use a Vintage Book

1A. Place the open cover facedown on a cutting mat.

1B. Position the metal ruler on the spine panel ¼ inch (6 mm) from the cover board. With a blade, cut the spine panel from the front cover by gently running the blade along the metal ruler. Reposition the ruler on the spine panel ¼ inch (6 mm) from the back cover board and repeat. (See the illustration on page 19.)

1C. To refine the cover boards, apply a thin coat of glue to the raw spine edges of one board using a glue brush. Fold the raw edge over the spine and press it to the back side of the board. Continue to apply pressure with your fingertips until the edge adheres to the board, or cover the front and back of the boards with wax paper and place them in a book press or beneath a stack of weights for a few minutes until they're dry.

Option 2: Use Binder's Board

2A. Use a paper cutter or utility knife with a metal ruler to cut two binder's boards to measure 4 x 6 inches (10.2 x 15.2 cm).

2B. Cover the boards with your choice of bookbinding cloth or paper, as instructed in Golden Picture Book (page 32).

MAKE THE TEXT BLOCK

3. Divide the writing paper into nine stacks of six sheets.

4. With your bone folder, fold each stack vertically into signatures measuring 4¼ x 11 inches (10.8 x 27.9 cm).

5. To determine the width for the signatures, measure the width of the front cover and subtract ⅛ inch (3 mm). To determine the signatures' height, measure the height of the front cover and subtract ¼ inch (6 mm). Use a paper cutter to cut the signatures to size.

6. Determine the dimensions of the end sheets; they will be the same height as the signature, and the width of the signature plus ¾ inch (1.9 cm). You should be able to cut both end sheets from one of the two sheets of decorative paper.

7. Cut two end sheets out of the decorative paper using the paper cutter.

8. Place the end sheets on the top page of the first signature and the back page of the final signature, with the extra width wrapping around the spine edges of the signatures. (See figure B on page 104.)

LINE THE COVERS

9. Measure and prepare the decorative paper that will cover the inside of the boards. (Again, you will cut both pieces from one sheet of decorative paper.) It should be cut to the same dimensions as your folded signature.

10. Lay one sheet facedown on a piece of wax paper.

11. Use a brush to apply a thin coat of glue to it.

12. Center the paper, glue side down, on the inside of a cover and smooth any bubbles with your bone folder.

13. Repeat for the remaining sheet and cover board.

PREPARE THE SPINE

14. Make a spine guide from Template 1.

15. Place the leather, front side up, on your work surface, and center the guide on top of the leather. Use a pencil to mark the holes and corner curves onto the leather.

16. Use the leather punch to punch the marked holes in the leather, and round the corners with scissors.

MAKE A PUNCH GUIDE FOR THE SIGNATURES

17. Determine the dimensions of the punch guide: It will be the same height as your signature and 4 inches (10.2 cm) wide. Cut the template to this size from the sheet of cardstock. Fold the guide in half lengthwise. Smooth the fold with your bone folder.

18. Open the template and place it on your work surface.

19. Measure ½ inch (1.3 cm) from the top and bottom of the guide, and use a pencil to mark the points along the fold. Measure ¾ inch (1.9 cm) inside the top and bottom marks and make points along the fold. Again, measure 1¼ inches (3.2 cm) inside the previous marks and mark along the fold. Determine the midpoint of the guide and mark that on the fold. Write "Signature 1, 9 Only" beside the center mark. See the Sample Template as a visual aid.

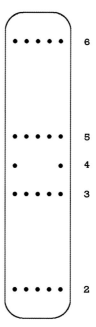

template 1
⅞ x 4 inches (2.2 x 10.2 cm)

Enlarge template by 20%

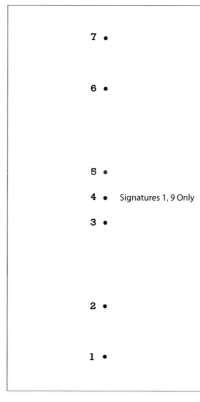

Signatures 1, 9 Only

sample template
3 x 5¾ inches (7.6 x 14.6 cm)

Enlarge template by 30%

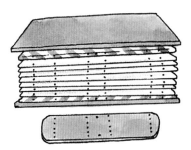

fig. A

fig. B

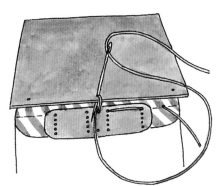

fig. C

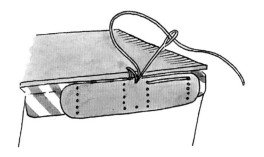

fig. D

PUNCH HOLES IN SIGNATURES

IMPORTANT: Only punch the center station for the first and last signature.

20. Nest the hole punch inside the center of each signature, set the signature in the gutter of an open phone book, and use an awl to punch the sewing stations.

21. After each signature is punched, arrange them into a text block.

PUNCH HOLES IN THE COVERS

22. Close the punch guide along the crease and align it with the spine edge of the front cover board. Center the guide between the top and bottom of the cover.

23. With a pencil, mark sewing stations 1, 4, and 7 on the cover, ¼ inch (6 mm) in from the spine edge. Repeat for the back cover. Use an awl to punch the marked holes on both covers. Each cover will have three holes.

PREPARE THE THREAD

24. Determine the amount of thread you'll need by multiplying the height of the front cover by nine, and then add 24 inches (61 cm). Measure this amount from your spool and cut.

25. If the thread is unwaxed, run the thread over a bar of beeswax. Thread the needle.

ASSEMBLE THE BOOK

26. Prepare the text block for binding. Make certain all pages are in order, including the end sheets. Place the text block inside the covers. Position the book front side up. Place the leather spine near the spine edge of the signatures (A).

27. Begin binding the book by pulling the top signature from the unbound book. Beginning with this signature, enter into sewing station 1 and pull the thread to the inside of the signature. Leave 12 inches (30.5 cm) of loose thread on the outside of the signature.

28. Enter into station 2 and pull the thread to the outside of the signature. Align the leather spine, and guide the needle through its top right hole (station 2). Pull the thread taut.

29. Enter into the next hole on the leather (station 3) and into the corresponding hole in the spine of the signature. Pull the thread to the inside of the signature and pull it tight to tighten the leather to the spine.

30. Enter through station 4 (the center station) and pull the thread to the outside of the signature and through the corresponding hole on the leather (B).

31. Place the top cover on the signature and align the center holes.

Pull the thread to the outside of the cover and enter into the center hole. Pull the thread through the cover hole. Repeat this a second time to make a double wrap around the cover spine (C).

32. Pull the thread to the outside of the leather spine and reenter the center station. Pull the thread to the inside of the signature (D).

33. Enter through station 5 from the inside of the signature, and pull the thread through the corresponding hole in the leather spine to the outside. Pull the thread taut.

34. Enter into the next hole (station 6). Pull the thread taut to the inside of the signature.

35. Enter into sewing station 7 from the inside of the signature, and pull the thread to the outside of the signature (E).

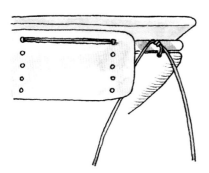

fig. E

36. Pull the next signature from the unbound book, place it next to the top signature and enter the needle into the nearest hole (station 7).

37. Continue binding the book using the same steps as above, with the following changes:

    SIGNATURES 2 through 8 do not have a center station or a cover, so skip steps 30–32.

    SIGNATURE 2 will share leather holes with signature 1 (F).

    SIGNATURES 3 and 4 will share the second row of leather holes.

    SIGNATURE 5 will have the third row of leather holes to itself.

    SIGNATURES 6 and 7 will share the fourth row of leather holes.

    SIGNATURES 8 and 9 will share the fifth row of leather holes.

    FOR signature 9, in the center hole follow step 31 to attach the remaining cover (G).

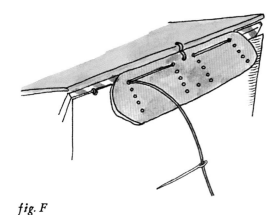

fig. F

REMEMBER to link all signatures at the top and bottom stations with a true kettle stitch; the only exceptions are when you do a direct link (page 140) between signature 1 and signature 2 at sewing station 7, and when you connect signatures 1 and 2 with a square knot at sewing station 1 (E).

38. Leave the thread long after the final kettle stitch. It will be used in the final step to attach the covers.

OPTIONAL: When sewing signatures 8 and 9, gather the threads of all previous signatures in stations 2 and 3 and stations 5 and 6 with a gathering stitch.

39. When the binding of the text block is complete, use the tails of the thread to attach the covers (see page 25).

40. Tie off (see page 27) inside the nearest signature.

TIP: If the finished binding is tight and causing the covers to lift open on their own, try placing the closed book in a book press or under a stack of heavy books or a weight to break in the binding. Keep it under the weight for a couple of hours, or until the cover rests naturally closed.

fig. G

OLD WORLD BOOK STRAP

This hand-crafted book strap is perfect for displaying or transporting three to five small books the Old World way.

stitch used

Decorative, instructed below

what you need

Basic Bookmaking Toolkit (page 13)

Small piece of cardstock

3- to 4-ounce (85 to 113.4 g) leather strap, 1 x 40 inches (2.5 x 101.6 cm)

2 metal D rings, 1 inch (2.5 cm)

Piece of cardboard, 4 x 4 inches square (10.2 x 10.2 cm)

1/32-inch (0.8 mm) leather punch

Binder's thread, 36 inches (91.4 cm)

1. Make a cardstock punch guide (see page 17) from Template 1.

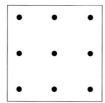

template 1
1 x 1 inch (2.5 x 2.5 cm)

2. Place the leather strap on your work surface with the back side facing up. Measure 2 inches (5.1 cm) from one end and draw a line with a pencil.

3. Place the D rings on the strap with the straight edges toward the back side of the leather. Position both rings at the 2-inch (5.1 cm) mark (A).

4. Fold the end of the leather to the back at the 2-inch mark so the rings are at the fold and the back sides are touching. Align the side edges of the strap.

5. Place the punch guide on the overlapping section of the strap and center it between the end of the strap and the folded edge that holds the D rings.

6. Place the cardboard under the end of the strap to protect your work surface.

7. Use an awl to mark the holes of the punch guide. Use enough pressure to penetrate both layers of the strap (B).

8. Unfold the strap and use the leather punch to punch through the marks on the leather, one layer at a time.

9. Place the D rings back in position, if necessary. Position the leather strap so the holes on both layers align.

10. With a single-threaded needle, enter into the center hole on the back of the strap (C).

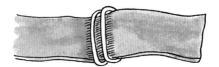

fig. A

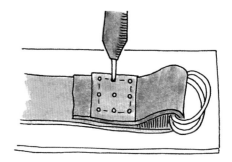

fig. B

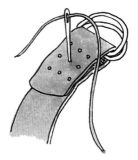

fig. C

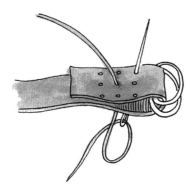

fig. D

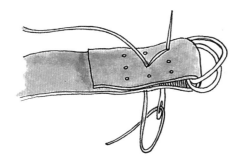

fig. E

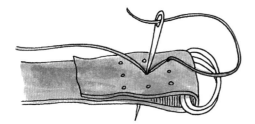

fig. F

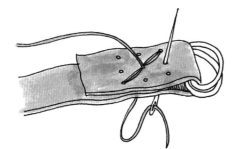

fig. G

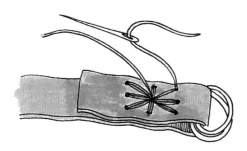

fig. H

11. Pull the needle through both layers of the strap and leave a tail of 4 inches (10.2 cm) on the back side.

12. Guide the needle into one of the outer holes from the front and pull the thread taut through both layers of strap to the back side (D). Enter into the center hole and pull the thread through to the other side again. Enter into the same outer hole as before (E) and pull thread taut. Return to the center hole with the thread and again pull taut (F). This makes a double stitch.

13. Repeat step 12 for each of the remaining outer holes (G). The order doesn't matter. Each hole will be wrapped around twice with the thread. Always return to the center hole (H).

14. Once all the holes are complete, tie off with a square knot (page 28) on the back side and trim the tails to ⅛ inch (3 mm).

BOOK OF REMINDERS

Is there something you don't want to forget?
Tie a string on it.

finished dimensions

3½ x 6 x 1 inches (8.9 x 15.2 x 2.5 cm)

stitch used

Running stitch (page 20)

what you need

Basic Bookmaking Toolkit (page 13)

Bookbinding thread, 56 inches (142 cm)

36 sheets of 70 lb. writing paper, 6½ x 5⅞ inches (16.5 x 14.9 cm)

2 decorative end sheets, 4 x 5⅞ inches (10.2 x 14.9 cm)

1 sheet of cardstock

1 ounce (28.4 g) of ¹⁄₆₄-inch (0.4 mm) or thinner leather, 10 x 8½ inches (25.4 x 21.6 cm)

¹⁄₁₆ (1.6 mm) Leather punch

2 binder's boards for the cover, 3⅜ x 6 inches (8.6 x 15.2 cm), ¹⁄₁₆ inch (1.6 mm) thick

Binder's board for the spine, ¾ x 6 inches (1.9 x 15.2 cm), ¹⁄₁₆ inch (1.6 mm) thick

Decorative sheet for lining the cover, 8½ x 11 inches (21.6 x 27.9 cm)

11 pieces of embroidery floss in several colors, each 8 inches (20.3 cm) long

MAKE THE TEXT BLOCK

1. Stack the sheets of writing paper into six groups of six. Use a bone folder to fold each stack in half to make signatures of 3¼ x 5⅞ inches (8.3 x 14.9 cm).

2. Add a decorative end sheet to the first signature. To do this, align one of the long edges of the end sheet to the open end of the first signature so it sits on top of the signature. The end sheet will be ½ inch (1.3 cm) wider than the signature. Fold the excess over the spine side of the signature (A). Repeat these steps to add the bottom end sheet to the last signature.

PUNCH THE SIGNATURES

3. Make a signature punch guide (page 17) from cardstock using Template 1. Nest the template in the centerfold of each signature, place the signature in the gutter of an open phone book, and punch the holes using an awl. Stack the signatures in order, and set them to the side.

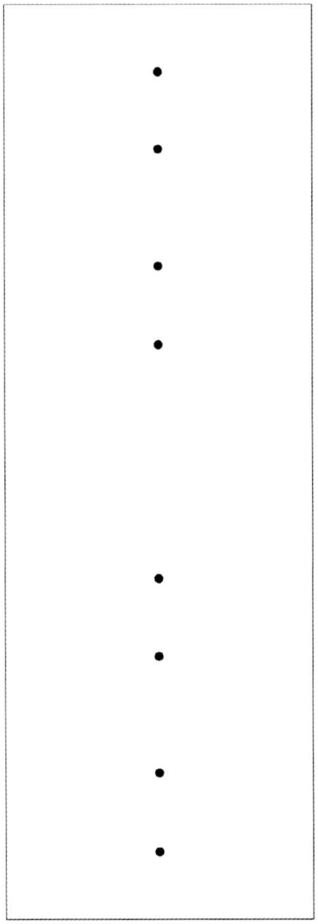

template 1
3 x 5⁷⁄₈ inches (7.6 x 14.9 cm)

Enlarge template by 20%

PUNCH THE SPINE

4. Make a spine punch guide from cardstock using Template 2, and center it on one side of the spine piece. Use a pencil to mark the holes onto the board. Use a hole punch to puncture the marks in the board.

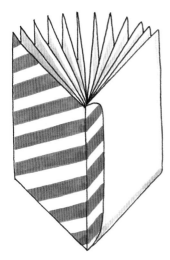

fig. A

template 2
¾ x 6 inches (1.9 x 15.2 cm)

Enlarge template by 20%

MAKE THE COVER

5. Cover your work surface with a 12 x 12-inch (30.5 x 30.5 cm) sheet of wax or craft paper.

6. Lay the leather back side up on top of the paper. Position the cover and the spine boards on the leather as shown in illustration B, leaving at least ¾ inch (1.9 cm) of space between the edge of the boards and the edge of the leather.

fig. B

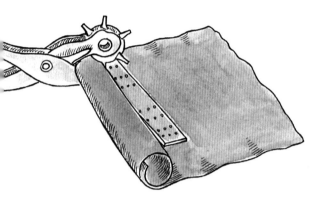

fig. C

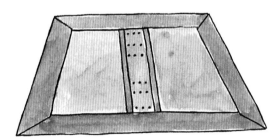

fig. E

7. Use a ruler to measure a ⅛-inch (3 mm) space between the spine board and each cover board, positioning all three of them so their top and bottom edges are aligned (B).

8. Hold the left cover board firmly on the leather and use a pencil to trace its edges onto the leather. Repeat for the spine and the remaining cover board.

9. Pick up the spine piece and use a brush to apply a thin layer of glue to one side. Place the spine, glue side down, onto the leather. Flip the leather over and smooth the spine area with a bone folder.

10. Use a leather punch to make the spine holes in the leather. If you are using a rotary punch, you may need to roll one of the leather covers toward the spine to access the holes (C). Unroll the leather when complete.

11. Apply a thin coat of glue to one side of one cover board. Place the glue side of the board within the marks on the leather. Flip the entire leather piece over and use a bone folder to smooth the leather to the board. Turn the leather over. Repeat for the remaining cover board.

12. Use the ruler to measure ¾ inch (1.9 cm) around the outer edges of the boards. Mark this distance with a pencil and use a metal ruler and pencil to connect all the marks, forming a square around the boards. Use scissors to cut away the leather outside the line.

13. Measure ⅛ inch (3 mm) from the four outer corners of the cover boards and mark with a pencil (D). Position a ruler diagonally across each mark and draw a line. Use scissors to trim the marks along all four corners, nipping them off.

14. Use a brush to apply a thin layer of glue to the entire bottom edge of the leather. Fold the leather up to meet the board. Use a bone folder to smooth the edge, pressing the leather onto the board and in the two gaps between the boards and spine. Repeat for the top edge. Repeat for the side edges (E).

15. Cut the decorative lining sheet in half, place the two sheets on the insides of the covers, and center them. The inside edges of the sheets will align with the raw inner edges of the cover boards. Use a brush to apply a thin coat of glue to the back side of one of the sheets. Adhere the sheet to the inner cover and use a bone folder to smooth. Repeat for the other lining sheet.

16. Use a leather punch to punch through the folded-over leather at the bottom and top holes of the spine.

ASSEMBLE THE BOOK

17. Position the cover so that it is open and the fore edge of the top cover is facing you. Place the text block near the cover with the spine facing you. Choose the bottom signature from the text block and place it on the back cover with the holes aligned.

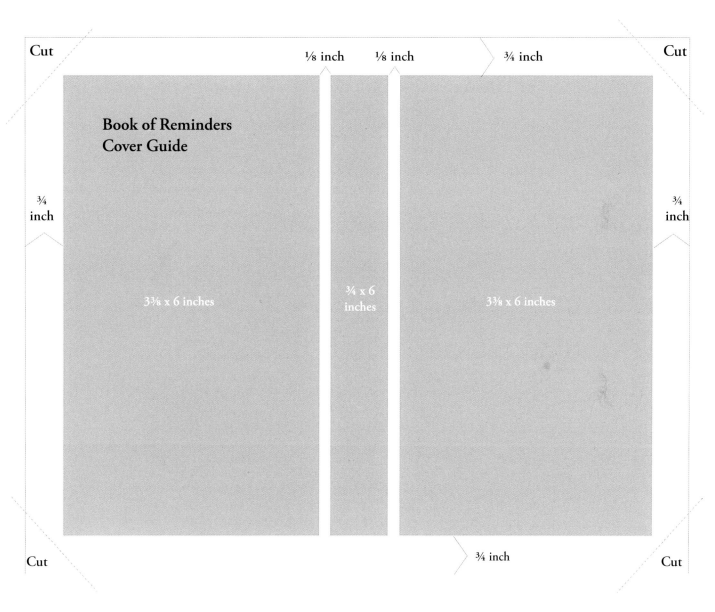

Cut

⅛ inch   ⅛ inch   ¾ inch

Cut

**Book of Reminders
Cover Guide**

¾
inch

¾
inch

3⅜ x 6 inches   ¾ x 6
inches

3⅜ x 6 inches

Cut   ¾ inch   Cut

fig. D

fig. F

18. Close the front cover to reveal the outside of the spine. With a single-threaded needle, enter into sewing station 1, going through the spine and the signature. Pull the thread into the center of the signature until a 6-inch (15.2 cm) tail remains on the outside of the spine. Draw the needle into sewing station 2 and pull the needle and thread to the outside of the spine. Continue sewing a running stitch until you arrive at the outside of the spine on the far left.

19. Pull the thread taut and guide the needle into the center hole at sewing station 6 (directly above the one the needle just came out of). Pull the thread to the inside of the cover until it's taut. Guide the needle underneath the signature to the right of the thread and pull the thread toward the top edge of the spine (F). Draw the thread toward the front cover and pull it taut.

20. Pull the next signature from the bottom of the stack and place it on top of the signature inside the cover. From the outside, guide the needle directly into sewing station 6 on the signature and pull it toward the inside until the thread is taut.

21. Guide the needle into the next sewing station to the right (station 5) and out through the aligning cover hole in the same row as the previous signature. (Since there are six signatures and only three rows of holes along the spine, every two signatures share a row.)

22. Pull the thread taut and continue sewing the signature and cover stations to the right with a running stitch until the thread is on the outer side of the cover's sewing station 1.

23. Directly enter into the center hole at station 1. Pull the next signature from the bottom of the stack and place it on top of the sewn signatures. Guide the thread into station 1 of the signature and draw the thread to the inside. Continue sewing with a running stitch to link the signature with the center row of stations on the cover's spine.

24. Once the thread is on the outside of the cover's center hole at station 6, draw the needle into the top hole at station 6 and pull it to the inside until it's taut.

25. Guide the needle underneath the nearest signature to the right of the thread like you did before (F), and pull the thread toward the edge of the spine. Draw the thread toward the front cover and pull it taut.

26. Pull the next signature from the bottom of the stack and place it on top of the signature inside the cover.

27. Guide the needle into sewing station 6 of the signature. Pull it taut and continue linking the signature to the cover with a running stitch until the thread is on the outside of the cover at station 1. This signature will share the same cover holes as the previous signature.

28. Guide the needle into station 1 of the top row and pull it to the inside of the cover. Pull the next signature from the bottom of the stack and place it on top of the signature inside the cover.

29. Guide the thread into sewing station 1 into the center of the signature. Continue linking the signature to the top row of the cover using a running stitch.

30. Once the thread is on the outside of the cover at station 6 (the top left hole), draw the needle directly into the hole below it (in the middle row). Pull the thread taut.

31. Draw the thread up and around the top of the signatures toward the final sewing station (signature sewing station 6). Place the remaining signature inside the cover and guide the needle directly into sewing station 6. Pull it taut.

32. Continue linking the signature to the cover with a running stitch until the thread is on the outside of the cover at station 1 in the top row.

33. To finish, guide the needle into station 1 in the center row of the cover and into station 1 on the nearest signature. Pull the thread to the center of the signature and tie off (page 000). Trim the thread to ¼ inch (6 mm). Thread the needle onto the remaining 6-inch (15.2 cm) tail and repeat this step.

ATTACH THE THREADS

34. Create a template from Template 3. Each signature will have a thread on the first page and the right-hand page of the centerfold. The only exception is the first signature, which will only have one on the centerfold. You will punch 11 holes total.

35. Begin with the centerfold of the first signature and align the template with the right edge of the right-hand page. Use a pencil to mark hole 1.5. Continue to the first page of the second signature, align the template, and mark hole 2. Continue through the signatures and mark the holes accordingly with only one mark per page.

36. Use the hole punch to punch all marks.

37. Draw one end of a length of embroidery floss through the first hole, loop around the edge of the page, and gently pull the ends until they meet. Hold both thread ends together and form a loose square knot (G).

38. Gently move the knot to meet the edge of the paper, then pull the ends to tighten. Use care so the paper does not tear. Trim the ends to 1½ inches (3.8 cm). Continue to the next signature and repeat the above steps.

Align to edge of page

1.5

2

2.5

3

3.5

4

4.5

5

5.5

6

6.5

template 3
1½ x 5⁷/₈ inches (3.8 x 14.9 cm)

Enlarge template by 20%

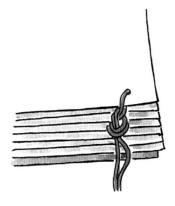

fig. G

BOOKMAKING TERMINOLOGY

AGAINST THE GRAIN, WITH THE GRAIN:
Refers to the direction the paper is folded. Against the grain is folding the paper at right angles to the grain. With the grain is folding the paper parallel to the grain. See *grain*.

CARDSTOCK, COVER STOCK:
A heavy paper used for making templates.

DIRECT LINK:
A technique used to link signatures that involves drawing the thread directly into an adjacent sewing station of the nearest signature without making a knot or stitch.

END SHEETS:
The sheets of paper (often decorative) located between the cover and the text block.

EXPOSED SPINE:
A bound spine that is not covered with material. Rather, both the text block and the stitching are visible, and the stitching is both decorative and functional to the structure of the book.

GRAIN:
Refers to the direction the fibers in the paper lie and is often considered when folding the paper into signatures. See *against the grain, with the grain*.

HEAD:
The top page edges or the top of the spine. See *tail*.

JOG:
To firmly hold a group of sheets or signatures together and knock one edge against a hard surface to align the individual edges.

LINK:
See direct link.

PAGE:
One side of a leaf. The number of sheets multiplied by four equals the number of pages in a book. See *sheet*.

PAMPHLET:
A booklet made one of signature or section.

SEWING STATIONS:
The pierced or punched holes along the fold of the signatures that hold the thread of the binding.

SHEET:
The full size of the paper before it is folded at the midline.

SIGNATURE, SECTION:
A group of nested folios that is comprised of eight or more pages. Technically, the word signature is a term used by printers, while section is used by binders. In this book, I use the term *signature*.

SPINE:
The bound edge of a book where the text block is stitched together with thread; the backbone of the book.

TAIL:
The bottom page edges or the bottom of the spine. See *head*.

TAPES:
Thick paper or cloth that is placed between one or more sewing stations on an exposed spine and is integrated into the binding to strengthen the structure of the book.

TEXT BLOCK:
The total compiled signatures of a book; in *Bound*, this includes the end sheets.

TIE OFF:
To complete the binding of the text block by drawing the tails of the thread into the sewing station of the nearest signature and fastening it to the thread inside with a square knot.

RESOURCES

Begin your search for materials and tools at your nearest locally owned art, craft, and thrift shops. Not only will your purchase support the livelihood of the local purveyors and employees, but you may also find a quicker, and sometimes less expensive, route to the best product by asking an experienced employee for recommendations. If a local shop doesn't carry what you're looking for, try checking out the following tried-and-true suppliers:

Bookbinding & Paper
Talas
Brooklyn, NY
www.talasonline.com

Hollanders
Ann Arbor, MI
www.hollanders.com

French Paper Co. (Made in USA)
Niles, MI
www.frenchpaper.com

Diamond Drill Bits
Rio Grande
Albuquerque, NM
www.riogrande.com

Leather, Snaps, Tools
Horween Leather (Made in USA)
Chicago, IL
www.horween.com & www.thetanneryrow.com

Tandy Leather
Worldwide
www.tandyleatherfactory.com

Zelikovitz Leathers & Crafts
Ontario, Canada
www.zelikovitz.com

ACKNOWLEDGMENTS

Thank you,

To my parents, for never telling me who I had to be and never questioning whom I've become.

To James Ferraris, for your patience and incredible capacity to take care of our children, our home, and myself during the making of this book.

To Kathleen McKafferty, for seeing the author in me.

To editors Becky Shipkowski, Thom O'Hearn, and John Foster, for your keen vision, support, and unfailing ability to fill in my blanks.

To art directors and designers Kathy Holmes, Kevin Ullrich, Jon Chaiet, and Rich Hazelton, for making *Bound* beautiful.

To Kathy Brock, for your keen eye to detail.

To Sue Havens, for your talent, patience, and gorgeous illustrations.

To Satya Curcio, for your friendship and beautiful translation of this book through your photography.

To Emily Aring, Libi Geddes, Nikki Ames, the Trading Company, James Infinity and Cathleen McCluskey, for your artful living and generosity in providing the space or props for the photo shoot.

To Carly James and Kevin Nelson of Bison Bookbinding & Letterpress, for waving me into your portal so many years ago and proving to me that the old world ways are long from lost.

To Elsi Vassdal Ellis, for impressing a love for book arts into my student mind. Your anthem "Any day with Book Arts is a good day" has become mine.

To all of you who've support Odelae by purchasing and commissioning books along the way: You've enabled me to live a life I love.

And to Orcas Island, for your elemental bounty, your wild poetry and your ever-arriving magic. I believe in You.

ABOUT THE AUTHOR

Photo by Satya Curcio Photography

Erica grew up on a remote prairie farm in South Dakota surrounded by family, animals, a scattering of cottonwood trees, and snow. Her love for books was kindled at a young age due to her grandmother Minnie's persistence that she be the one to teach her granddaughter to read. Erica went on to win spelling bees, reading and essay competitions, and eventually ran out of books to read in the nearby town library. In the years that followed, she wandered and plucked from the aisles of more than a couple different university libraries while studying architecture, literature, sustainability, and art. During that time, she received her first bookbinding lesson. In 2004 she accepted a BA in Graphic Design and headed to the forested foot of Mt. Baker, WA, where she discovered that bookbinding was more than a pastime. Today, she continues to live close to nature in the Pacific Northwest with her sweetheart and their two children. Her work as a bookbinder and graphic designer is influenced by nature, folk tales from around the world, and the faded, timeworn materials that survive from the early 1900s. She sells her books online at www.odelae.com and keeps shop on Etsy at www.odelae.etsy.com.

INDEX